ALSO BY NANI POWER

Crawling at Night
The Good Remains
The Sea of Tears

Feed the Hungry

A Memoir, with Recipes

Nani Power

Free Press
New York London Toronto Sydney

*f*P
Free Press
A Division of Simon & Schuster, Inc.
1230 Avenue of the Americas
New York, NY 10020

Note to Readers:

Names of certain people & places portrayed in this book have been changed.

First Free Press hardcover edition April 2008

FREE PRESS and colophon are trademarks of Simon & Schuster, Inc.

For information about special discounts for bulk purchases,
please contact Simon & Schuster Special Sales at 1-800-456-6798 or
business@simonandschuster.com

Book design by Ellen R. Sasahara

Manufactured in the United States of America

10   9   8   7   6   5   4   3   2   1

Library of Congress Cataloging-in-Publication Data

Power, Nani.
    Feed the hungry: a memoir, with recipes / Nani Power.
        p. cm.
        1. Power, Nani.   2. Power, Nani—Family.   3. Power, Nani—
knowledge—Food.   4. Power, Nani—Travel.   5. Authors, American—
20th century—Biography.   I. Title.
PS3566.O83577Z46   2008
813'.54—dc22   2007045503

ISBN-13: 978-1-4165-5606-0
ISBN-10:   1-4165-5606-0

Contents

Contents

Contents

Prologue

A Memoir, with Recipes

This is a book about hunger. You could call it long-ing, in a more poetic sense, but hunger implies a physical need, an instinctual force that is relentless. It is a daily reminder of our bodies, but it is also the invisible chain that threads our memories to our heart, insistent and throbbing, woven of culture and nostalgia.

The constant running theme of my family—part bohemian dreamers, part southern aristocracy—and its demise will be the *trunk* of the book, the travel memories will be various *branches* of my adult life that evolved from my earlier life. This is my attempt, through the journey of the stomach, to make sense of all my feelings regarding being a member of a clan of eccentrics.

In the end, it's a hunger for the purity of experience. As human beings, it is our common connection to the animal, driving us back to the physical. We can satisfy this simply, in a basic way, or in all sorts of fancy embellishments, meant to soothe various hungers at the same time. I see my family as a cluster of entertaining, charming sorts thrown together in a haphazard way, loosely threaded, buffeted by the winds of life, starving for everything they can get. In the end, no one walked away sated and full, but quietly starved in different worlds, like tented refugees with one small bag of rice, still hungering.

And then, between these stories, come tales of how I navigate in this world. In a culture unfamiliar, I want to trade the hot, resinous air of the airport quickly for the damp and smelly market, the cafés, the roadside stands. After a trip, you are ravenous, tired, worn. You've eaten horrible mini pretzels as if they were niblets of foie gras, you've recrossed your legs a thousand times, silently fought like Xerxes for Athens over the tiny sliver of space undefined by the seat armrest, seen an obscured and badly wrought romantic comedy on a tiny screen, fantasy-ordered umpteen odd gadgets from the airline catalogue—in essence you've compressed and redefined yourself willingly for ten-odd hours on the assumption the future reward will be great. That you will emerge from the giant metal cocoon and find originality. It is through the senses an artist perceives the world, and what more gloriously invites the senses than great food? My grandfather's tales of Machu Picchu and flocks of wild parrots led me there years later, chewing coca leaves in the early morning mist. My mother giving me tuna sashimi when I was ten, and sushi was largely unheard of, led me to Tokyo and the icy fish market at four A.M., to the genesis of *Crawling at Night*, my first novel, in which I introduced Katsuyuki Ito, an estranged sushi chef in Manhattan.

Hunger gives us a regular sensation we can rely on, and food is the satisfaction of our needs, at least for now. It is the hunger that permeates us in a more elusive sense, beyond our daily lives, the gnawing of our spirit, which is harder to accommodate.

Most of arc us are walking, starving ghosts, seeking a good meal.

Feed the Hungry

Chapter 1

Virginia

The Dogs Bark but the Caravan Moves On, 1961–1971

In the first place, there is hunger, sniffing like a restless night beast toward satisfaction. To the kitchen in the cold night or bars on the edge of town, to the shiny mall, to new loves, new cars, new music! New anything! The drive is relentless. Is it the hunger of the stomach, but it has spiritual repercussions as well. Where is the difference between an actual instinct and a vague malaise? The growl of the stomach becomes the ache of the heart, becomes the screech of the banshee, the warrior's yell, the beat of the Mongol's drum, a song of vengeance. It could be a lot of songs, but it has only a small tune hummed ceaselessly, repetitively: hunger, deep and gnawing.

This is the title of the first book I ever wrote: *Small Delicacies for Ladies*. I was ten. In the few pages of this unfinished classic, I managed to provide a long, tediously wrought recipe for candied violets and mint leaves, both of which I was fond of making. I learned these recipes from an ancient tome I found in the home of my eccentric grandparents, Francis and Mary, who lived on a sprawling farm in rural Virginia. These were my father's parents, and although my parents divorced when I was young, we would make regular forays to their house. Their kitchen was dank and cool, lying partially underground, with a varnished brick floor. One had to go down the stairs from the upstairs hall, as if going into a dark basement. On the old stone and stucco walls, Francis had painted old medieval shields and figures, old crests and daggers. The smell was earthy stone and a healthy waft of moss. In general, one felt an unconscious surge as one came down the stairs, a Jungian journey into something unspoken and magical. From the kitchen one could enter the outdoor covered porch, laid in smooth obsidian stone and decorated with ancient Hindu statues and various decaying wicker furniture cluttered around a large lawn. Masses of stalky mint squeezed from the edge of the columns, and violets dotted the lawn, and here I gathered my sources of the delicacies.

The mint leaves were tricky, you had to carefully wash them of dust in just a mist of cold water and dry them on paper towels. I didn't even bother washing the violets, as they would no doubt disintegrate quickly into a purple mush. I boiled some sugar and water for about six minutes until the mixture thickened slightly and bubbled in a slow, unctuous way, like lava. You quickly dipped each leaf or violet in the goo and laid them out on foil to dry. You could use chopsticks or tiny tongs. I think I used my fingers and I think I got burned. I seem to remember the distinct sensation of candied fingertip, red, caustic, and sweet. After the leaves dried quite rapidly, they became tiny surreal jewels. They were bright and glittery and crackled against each other like fall leaves. My two half sisters, younger than me, were enchanted by them and we ate them on the lawn, overlooking a large brown river way across the meadow, where occasional shaggy horses strolled about.

I'm not sure what Francis and Mary did exactly, but they didn't farm directly. A grizzled old-timer named Eugene Stephenson did that. They were dilettantes. They seemed to play, as we did. Mary had a puzzle of a million pieces always set on a table upstairs and she sometimes played with that, or she slept in the afternoons, or she sat in a chair on the lawn with her white curled hair and dark small glasses, laughing with visitors.

Francis had gone to Yale, studied architecture. He painted, cooked the occasional *blanquette de veau*, drank, smoked tiny cigars, wore ascots, and had built a gothic prayer room in a hall closet. He was quite handsome and it was rumored that he kept a woman in Washington, D.C. It was said he was writing a book on stone church architecture. He had published one novel, a thriller, called *The Encounter* under the pen name of Crawford Power.

Their kitchen, as I mentioned, was underground and seemed dug from cool stone. It was the kitchen of a mossy ancient castle or a thousand-year-old cave. No doubt this imparted a certain metaphysical languor to cooking, as if one was engaged in dru-idish rites of magic or alchemy. Upstairs in my grandfather's study, he kept a human skull. The cookbooks were old and dusty, lounging on ramshackle shelves in the kitchen, contain-ing recipes no one made anymore. A small needlepoint on the wall said *The dogs bark but the caravan moves on*. I had nothing really to do when I visited but read or cook. Occasionally, I drew. I remember cooking lots of things in that kitchen, the candied items, then later on, as an adult, I made a special dinner for my father, who had moved in after my grandparents died—Mary from intestinal cancer, Francis from a heart attack. Instantly, the tone of the house grew lighter, airier. Mark, my father, replaced the blackamoors and heavy Victorian artifacts with his vast collection of photos—being a quite accomplished artistic photographer by trade. This meal was made for him and some of his best photographic cronies, charming men surrounding themselves in a perpetual spasm of clicking and flashing, as if time itself had to be recorded and studied before it eased away.

The meal was ornate and special for fall: I remember it as spiced butternut squash soup, followed by roast rack of lamb with an Indian onion chutney with curry leaves. The chutney is a wonderful thing, classically served with idlis, the steamed rice snack cakes of southern India, but is a great sauce for meats or sandwiches. You slow-cook the onions with mustard seeds and add the curry leaves at the last moment. You can find those in Asian or Indian markets, though I've even seen them in some of the upscale markets, like Wegmans. They have no flavor of curry, but impart a certain earthy muskiness, which complimented the pleasurable tomb-like quality of my grandfather's kitchen. I forgot what dessert I made, but if I were doing this menu now, fall resplendent outside, ochered and toasty warm, I would follow with a local persimmon Pavlova and sprinkle with candied mint leaves, in honor of nostalgia. There are a few wild persimmon trees on the property, gnarled things, which produced a mass of opaque gilden fruits that must be iced by the first frost in order to transform from a hideous mouth-wrenching pucker to velvetlike custard. It's their color which is so lovely—pearlized coral, or gauzed apricot.

The skin, unlike commercial varieties, is ultra thin and crepey, like the upper arm of an eighty-year-old woman. They are mostly pit, so you have to use quite a few. They were one of first fruits discovered in Virginia. Captain John Smith of Jamestown (a relative, actually), wrote: "The fruit is like a medlar; it is first green then yellow, and red when ripe; if not ripe, it will drive a man's mouth awry with much torment; but when it is ripe, it is as delicious as an apricock."

I seem to remember grandfather Francis as being quite a good cook, but obviously this was a youthful invention. My sister Shelagh recalls visiting with school friends to find him dining alone at the end of his grand mahogany table on curried bananas. I asked my father for information on Francis's culinary expertise, whereupon he produced a dry snort, mumbling something about how he'd boil everything down for hours into an intense essence. He added, though, that he tended to cook this way as well, and that "once your grandfather had the plate before him, he would go into a whirlwind of activity with the salt and pepper, a vicious sprinkling of salt over food and table and many grinds of the pepper mill. And then he would eat with relish. It must be genetic because I am pretty much the same. Virginia often chides me for throwing in too many ingredients and thus ruining simple, good food. The last time I think she objected to nutmeg in my scalloped potatoes. I have noted the subtlety in your cooking and even attempted to emulate it but then I see some dried figs in the pantry and think, hey, those would be good in this lentil dal. I cooked some chopped up rhubarb with ground lamb the other day and I don't care what anyone says, it was good. But the figs texturally were a bit surprising, the seeds like little explosions. But the flavor was good! Both your grandfather and I don't have subtle palates and I think that's the explanation. Years of smoking and in his case, smoking and drinking, have dulled our palates to the point where we have to jump-start our food, which causes those with normal palates to recoil in horror, especially when they find out what was in a particular dish."

Later though, he sent me a raccoon recipe with the following description: "The raccoon recipe was inspired by a night in which Eugene Stephenson, the farmer renting our farmland, invited us to tag along during one of his many nocturnal coon hunts. It was a memorable night. First of all, Gene began the hunt mounted on an albino mule, I think it was albino, I know it was white. Off he and the mule sauntered while the rest of us, not possessing mules, albino or otherwise, followed on foot. Us included the dog handler, by the name of Casey. Casey was a wizened old man about five feet tall who had the unenviable job of keeping ten dogs on the leash. Suddenly a white shape loomed up then vanished: the mule, sans Gene. I'm over here, he bellowed; he was now on foot, apparently being too drunk for continued equestrianship. Bring the dogs up, Casey, he commanded from somewhere in the underbrush. Now I could swear that the minute he heard this request, Casey went skyward, launched by the combined effort of ten dogs to reach their master. I do know for a fact he lost his footing and was dragged several feet over the ground by the eager beasts before he had the sense to let them go. The rest of the night, a confused blur of firefly lanterns, crashing through weeds, avoiding baying dogs and and stampeding cows, and finally gathering below a tree in which was a coon, is pretty much described in the recipe."

See recipe on page 16.

Certainly, Francis was an aesthete who lived elegantly in a

certain timeless bubble. I was around him here and there in my
childhood, absorbing from his gregarious hugs on my arrival a
crush of many scents: good leather, the bright limey tang of alcohol, and a smothering of warm patchouli, one of his many
blends of perfume he concocted himself. The house frightened
us, ancient and stiff with odd antiques, blackamoors, and that
horrible human skull. We children made our arrivals, fairly
unnoticed. We'd attack the puzzle table on the back sunroom
or loll in the cold algaed pool. He was one of the many colorful
characters who bespeckled my childhood, and then, when I
grew old enough to actually look at them with observant
eyes, seemed to fade like a distant star enveloped in black sky:
when finally gone, they exist as a dream, something invented
from another era, certainly not of this time. Who wears ascots
anymore?

In just a few miles from the sprawling medieval farm in the
Virginia countryside, lived my other grandparents, Gene and
Nancy, in an estate called Crednal in the pompous town of
Middleburg, noted for parlaying to the Kennedys and other
aristocrati devoted to equine interests. Oddly, they happened to
be the best friends of the aforementioned Francis and Mary,
and as proclivity would have it, I came out of the mix. Their
house was grander and decorated in early sixties southern sim-
plicity, some rattan here, a piece of chintz there, except for the
sequestered parlor, an ornate mausoleum of satin loveseats and
dog sculptures reserved only for guests. The aura of their
kitchen possessed none of the mystical haze of Mary and Francis's gypsy cave: this was a small factory mandated by a stately
black woman named Bertha, who cooked large amounts of

traditional Virginia fare, slow-cooked buttery lima beans, fried chicken, a wonderful beef vegetable soup with a layer of red fat and a swirl of local products, corn, peas, the ubiquitous lima beans. There was batter bread, cornbread, and popovers. I remember a multilayered cake, with perhaps ten thin layers oozing with icing. One fine day, it was sitting on a pantry and I thought she had layered pancakes in a surprising new way. My mother claims this is a Lady Baltimore cake. I beg to differ: I looked it up and found it is a Smith Island cake from Maryland. But Bertha made Lady Baltimore as well, a white cake studded with nuts and dried fruits. Occasionally, though, Bertha left the premises and my grandmother was the cook, and strangely, it's these meals I remember most. I say that because everyone rather secretly felt these were a definite step down from Bertha's brilliance, because Nancy didn't like to cook.

Nancy had a leonine cool blondness, hinting of the South and that moody ambiance without a twang or any of its unsavoriness. She would sit with her long limbs casually draped in front of her, cardigan, chin-length blond crimped hair. She came from an old Virginia family that was doing quite well until hit by the Depression. She seemed to have an inordinate amount of maiden aunts hanging around, as all those old families did. There was that miffed, residual irritation that hung around from the loss of the Civil War, as if someone had forgotten how to be gentlemen, in a big way. Some wouldn't even call it the Civil War, preferring the War Between the States. Two of her unmarried aunts, Beck and Mariah, actually had taken a ride with some friends in a new car, but when they found out it was a Lincoln, they declared they would need to be taken home. Those two aunts basically ran everything in the house. They picked the meals and raised young Nancy. She was forbidden to use the word "sweetbreads," which still confuses her to this day. The Depression hit them all hard. Nancy to this day must have a year's supply of toilet paper in the house because her family couldn't afford it and had to use newspaper. And yet, Henry, her father, and her mother, Mabel, scraped every bit, sold jewelry, and stock to mold together a precious $150 for the last cause, the ultimate sacrifice, for Nancy, to do well and have a debutante party in Washington.

At one of these many socialite whirlwinds that she fell into in those days, while visiting Princeton actually, she met Gene on a blind date. She told me he met her at the train station drunk as a skunk. Somehow they managed to stay together for sixty years. When she wasn't lipsticked and laughing and drinking gin, she was lounging on her large king-size bed, writing novels as well. So cooking the inevitable meal for her crowd—which was at that time my brother, John, my mother, Ann, and I (we had moved into a small house on the estate after a divorce), my two uncles, Harrison and Owen, and an odd friend or two—became a necessity. She would find one dish and work it for years. Lasagna was one of these. Next, marinated steak in bottled Italian dressing, cooked until gray, cut with the shredding implement of the seventies, the electric knife. And then, a wild chicken dish in a casserole involving a jar of apricot preserves. As plebeian as these were, I found them delicious.

We grew to endure more and more of these meals, because of the events of one particular day. My mother and uncle liked to sit in the kitchen and talk to Bertha. My brother and I liked to stay in the downstairs "mudroom" and watch *I Love Lucy* and *Petticoat Junction* and eat forbidden snacks that my hippie granola-baking mother wouldn't allow—Reese's Peanut Butter Cups and Vienna sausages in the can. One day, though, the cantilevered doors to the mudroom became swiftly shut and we were told to stay put. We peeked through the doors and saw what looked like Harrison, our uncle, kissing Bertha as she lay on the floor. Something was not right. After a while, an ambulance came and she was taken away. Later, it turned out that Bertha had said to my uncle, *Harrison, get me a chair for my leg, it has fallen asleep*, and then that was it, she was down. A stroke.

We fared for ourselves, after that. Gone were the golden days. My teenage uncle, Owen, burned huge three-pound steaks he charged to Nancy and Gene at the local butcher, and drizzled them with his "secret" recipe sauce, as he put it, which was merely lemon and butter. I went nuts on the Vienna sausage cans. A strange food anarchy hit Crednal. Alcohol seemed to become a new nutrition source. I remember Nancy becoming loopy and sentimental almost nightly after a couple of drinks, and my uncle Harrison's irritation at it all. In these wild times, I was allowed to swig a bit of champagne, make an attempt at a flowery toast, and fling the glass in the fireplace with a great, delightful spray of glass. My grandmother even bought six-packs of shrimp cocktail in the tiny glasses, with little metal lids you pried open, mainly for the purpose of smashing during toasts. There were also a bunch of industrial wine glasses from the Lone Oak Country Club thrown in, as an alternative group. The apricot chicken made more and more appearances. In other words, we got down to the bare nub.

My mother, however, was doing her own culinary Hippie's Tour of the World. In her long Mexican dresses, beads, her

Cherlike mop of brown hair with bangs, she was baking granola, making Hungarian goulash, cannolini, fondue. She'd
overkill on her latest, feeding us renditions until we fell in love
with the dish, then, never again would she make it. In some
odd sense of nostalgia for the three weeks in November 1968
when she perfected them, she's started making the old cannelloni again, mortadella sausage, veal, spinach wrapped in homemade crêpes, a soothing nutmeg-flecked béchamel. My older
uncle Harrison was on a wildlife foraging mission, hunting
and fishing in every corner of the land, bringing back deer, rabbits, dove, elk, bluegill, trout, bass. He even shot a bear once
and we baked a haunch of it, a massive, fulvous hunk covered
in grease as thick as Vaseline. Somehow one of the Labradors
that swarmed in a pack around the house devoured the meat
and convalesced for four days under a couch. The hunting had
little to do with food, it seemed he rather enjoyed the sport of
tracking things down and killing them. My brother joined him
on these forays. They shot skeet on cold fall mornings, with
various local friends. When he wasn't hunting, he enjoyed tor-
turing us or teasing. He had a game where he'd walk into a
room, scream *Assume the Fetal Position!* and we had to fling
ourselves to the ground in a ball in five seconds. Anyone who
lost received an Indian burn or some such pain. He also invented the Houdini Game, much to the delight of my family.
My brother or I would be tied to a chair, and timed to see how
quickly we could get out. Then, there was Operation. We'd
lie on the wooden bar, pushing aside the giant gallon jugs of
Bombay Gin, and Harrison would stick the wine opener in our
nose or ear or some such. We actually enjoyed these dracon-
ian games. They seem a little sick and bizarre in our world
now. The soundtrack to all these times was supplied by Owen,

the younger uncle, famous for playing songs over and over ad nauseum. How many times I heard "I Am the Walrus" as I ate the apricot chicken? or Mick Jagger's twang of "Paint It Black" as Harrison probed our inner ear with an icepick during Operation?

My older uncle Harrison had a dark and mocking nature. Every winter we went to a small island in the Bahamas and all stayed for two weeks. Oh, during this time we traded Bertha for the small and ill-tempered Carrie, who was later replaced by Muriel, who drank too much and saw little people in the kitchen. But, in between the foul moods and the drinking, they made stuffed crawfish and cracked conch and we never ate better. My family befriended the local English doctors, named Cants, and their large family of teenagers soon took over our house. My uncle somehow told one of them that back in Virginia we were the members of an odd satanic cult. Apparently, he believed him for years. And one day, he called up and was coming to visit. An elaborate plan was hatched. He was led blindfolded across a cornfield at night to my mother's small house, lit from within by candles and greeted by shrouded figures (my other uncle, us, friends all in on the gag). The heart of a small dove that Harrison had shot that day was put in his palms and he was told to eat it. At some point, when it seemed he would actually eat the thing, the place broke into laughter and the story stayed for years in the annals of our family. My uncle also told my brother and I that Boo Radley lived in the attic. I once ventured there, it was announced by a lilliputian set of stairs spiraling upward into darkness. Upon cracking open the door, I saw a windowless room, heavily scented with the warmth of sweat, a single bed neatly made, and a laundry rack with a series of putty-colored tights drying. It was Bertha's room. No Boo Radley, but it was scary still the same.

What was I doing through all of this? I was sitting in my room, drawing endless pictures of ladies in whimsical, extravagant costumes that I intended to make one day. I was writing stories and poems. My brother was off with Uncle Harrison pillaging the forests of wildlife or lost in some imaginary war game. One day I looked out my window and saw him with a plastic rifle, saying to no one, *Let's go, men.* Somehow, just out of boredom and maybe hunger, I started reading cookbooks, which seemed like fantasies of other worlds. They'd say things like *This is Aunt Miriam's favorite. Thanksgiving is just not the same without squirrel pie*, and one could envision the whole family, the voices, the food, their lives. Or, even better, because my family seemed to love the exotic, *This fish stew is served on the beach, on banana leaves. I recommend it served with dark rum and fresh Persian lime.* It became an escape, reading cookbooks.

Most of the time, however, I was trying to avoid my younger uncle, who although I adored him with his Beatles and Rolling Stones and fashionable mop of long hair, had suddenly changed. It was the height of the sixties and Owen was ripely in the midst of it all. He brought us The Beatles and The Rolling Stones, and we all loved it. Even my grandfather Gene, who favored crooning from the thirties like Cole Porter, had to admit "Yesterday" wasn't bad. Owen was closer to my age than Harrison, and nicer. He seemed to enjoy hanging out with us youngsters, laughing, clowning around. But in the way clouds move across the sky, in the softest yet perceptible way, he was growing increasingly odder and odder, and it seemed only I knew. I couldn't figure out what had happened to him, but he was changed—a subtle difference I couldn't have expressed even if I had been brave enough to do so. I tried to avoid him, but I had no tangible reason. When my mother or grandmother wanted to run off to the store, which was fine before, I balked. My brother didn't mind, he didn't see yet. I'd beg to go with them and they just thought I was being foolish. So, I'd watch them drive off down the long gravel driveway surrounded by boxwoods in fear, not knowing what he'd do. It didn't seem good.

Nobody noticed the change, like I said, but it was inevitable they would, and in fact, it became quickly obvious, with the arrival of his girlfriend's parents and the police at the door one sad, cold night when they claimed he had assaulted her. That night had begun a long road of denial and pain for my grandparents, until years later when they came to accept the fate of schizophrenia for poor Owen, who has lived in a mental ward most of his life. But what caused it? He had a bad car accident at eighteen, suffering a concussion and briefly going into a coma. I remember the whole thing dimly, as if etched in velvet. Some of us attribute this. But no one knows these things. He simply went away.

And, coincidentally, Francis and Mary suffered the same. Was it something in the water? Their son, my uncle as well, also had the same illness. It was Francis's unfortunate fate to discover his son's body one day, by that large river I mentioned that I looked upon while munching candied mint leaves, where he had taken his own life with a shotgun on a weekend visit from the hospital. Perhaps this is the silent bond written in some genetic code that brought these two families together so long ago. I suppose the definition of the illness could be the definition of our families even, removed from reality, living in a different world. Other children at school seemed to be from an alternative universe. Their lunch boxes held white bread and peanut butter and jelly, or bologna, or a pale, floppy version of ham with American cheese. The ham we ate at home was a dried, salty thing that took three days to cook and was served paper thin on Bertha's rolls. It would rest for days in the cold room wrapped in cheesecloth, where we could peel off slivers and eat it with bread and butter pickles. My lunches were often Roquefort cheese and Euphrates crackers, a popular choice for seven-year-olds. The other children also didn't seem to live in a small hippie cabin next to their grandparents, with mattresses on the floor, a giant hewn log for a coffee table and Bob Dylan playing until all hours. Their parents didn't wear beads, or take them to antiwar rallies, or smoke pot against their children's wishes.

It's like this: Up in the attic, beyond Bertha's room, there was a dusty airless room full of wooden crates, each seemingly full of goods and artifacts of the family through the years. *Those are Great-Aunt Beck's dresses*, my mother told me when we looked through a pile of ancient clothing from the eighteen hundreds, with large poufed sleeves, and ruffles and lace, bodices and petticoats, they all delighted me. But as you examined them, they crumbled in your hands. Sleeves fell off by threads and moths flew out. There were old books, family daguerreotypes in silver frames, Victorian furniture. Slowly, the clothing disintegrated into odd hunks and pieces, useless, yet somehow too valuable to throw away. And finally, everything fell apart: mice inhabited the eaves and took over, infiltrating the boxes with fluff and rattling dung. In the end it was all tossed out.

The curious hodgepodge of memory feels the same: hunks

of incidences tempered by vague recollection. A certain wail of the Beatles humming over a taxi's radio or the whiff of patchouli or the taste of a long-forgotten food brings back via the feelings a long-lost flash. It hits you in the stomach, the place you are fed, and swells to a high pitch of what the Brazilians seem to understand well, *saudade*, a mix of memory, regret, and homesickness. In that very instant, you are gifted the reprisal of wholeness—similar to Great-Aunt Beck's voluminous velvet dress in perfect condition—and if you can stay with it, hold it, handle it, you are there again in your childhood, before the instant it crumbles.

The recipe is a tool of continuity, a mystical thing, a stitch against the crumble. This book contains many of them, small hybrids of many worlds, tiny windows in that windowless attic of nostalgia.

Forthwith, Mark Power's Coon Recipe:

❖ Raccoon Goose Creek

This recipe, like all coon recipes, traditionally starts with the words, "Shoot, skin, gut & cover a medium-sized coon in saltwater . . ."

1. Shoot, skin, gut & cover a medium-sized coon in saltwater.
2. Add cut-up onions, potatoes, carrots, and celery, and soak overnight. Many times we have left out the overnight part. One time we even left out the coon. Save a cup of the liquid for sauce.
3. Dust coon lightly in flour & brown in skillet. Cut up if too big. A chainsaw does a quick job of it.
4. Make a gravy using ½ C brine-blood, ½ C sherry, ½ C beef broth, ½ C soy sauce as the liquid base.

5. Stuff chest cavity with carrots, potatoes, onions & scatter the vegetables around the beast.
6. Bake 3 hrs or to taste in a 375°F oven. For years, Eugene would leave out the cooking part. After they were married, his new wife Malvinia introduced him to the novelty of cooked food.

ps # 1. Anyone who first microwaves a coon let me know so I can add it to the recipe. Once we cooked one on a car radiator while driving from Snickersville, W.Va. to Rain Hole, Wisconsin. It was good despite nuances of 10–40 wt.

ps # 2. How to get a coon: go out in a pasture late at night with a pickup truck, a bottle of whiskey, one teen-age boy, ten dogs, & an equal number of friends. Once dogs tree coon, send teen-age boy up tree to shake animal down to ground. Stomp dogs & shoot coon, being careful not to shoot boy if he falls on ground next to coon which can happen. Skin at night in back of pickup with flashlight & a rusty penknife. As everyone knows skinning a coon does a good job of cleaning off rust.

Start soaking coon before you go to bed so you can cook animal in morning.

If it tastes like pork you may have cooked boy by mistake. Keep in mind coon should taste like coon not pork.

❖ Candied Mint Leaves

Select crisp, fresh mint leaves. Wash lightly in cold water and dry completely on paper towels. Put 1 cup sugar in a pan and add ½ cup water and ¼ cup light corn syrup. Boil without stirring for about 10 minutes, or until liquid turns slightly yellow or a candy thermometer reaches 310°F. Using tweezers, dip mint leaves quickly in the syrup and place on foil-lined baking sheets to dry.

❧ Rack of Lamb with South Indian Onion Chutney

2 tablespoons minced garlic
2 tablespoons chopped fresh rosemary
2 teaspoons salt
1¼ teaspoons black pepper
4 tablespoons olive oil
One 7-bone rack of lamb, trimmed and frenched
South Indian Onion Chutney (see below)

Preheat oven to 450°F. Move oven rack to center position. In large bowl, combine garlic, rosemary, 1 teaspoon of the salt, and ¼ teaspoon of the pepper. Toss in 2 tablespoons of the olive oil to moisten mixture. Set aside.

Season the rack all over with remaining 1 teaspoon salt and 1 teaspoon pepper. Heat remaining 2 tablespoons olive oil in a large heavy ovenproof skillet over high heat. Sear rack for 1 to 2 minutes on both sides. Set aside for a few minutes. Roll the rack in garlic-rosemary mixture until evenly coated. Cover the ends of the bones with foil to prevent charring.

Place the rack bone side down in the skillet. Roast the rack for 12 to 18 minutes, or until springy to the touch (medium rare). Using a meat thermometer, take a reading in the center of the meat after 10 to 12 minutes. Remove the meat, or let it cook longer, to your taste. Let the rack rest for 5 to 7 minutes, loosely covered with aluminum foil, before carving between the ribs. Serve with onion chutney.

❧ South Indian Onion Chutney

1 tablespoon vegetable oil
¼ cup chopped white onion
4 dried red chiles, seeded and chopped
1-inch-piece, ginger grated

Virginia

1 tablespoon tamarind concentrate
3 to 4 curry leaves
Salt to taste

Heat oil in skillet and sauté onion till translucent. Mix the sautéed onion with remaining ingredients and blend to a smooth paste in a blender. The chutney is ready to be served.

Chapter 2

Harbour Island

Blue Skies and Yellow Birds, 1969

I n December, my brother and I were woken at dawn, thrown in the car in blankets, half asleep, you watched the cerulean sky from a corner of the window, adult voices coming in waves from the front. We had been hijacked by my my young mother, a divorcee, and the usual group—grandparents Nancy and Gene, uncles Owen and Harrison.

Next came the plasticine odor of the plane, the mangling of space, *Let me take you down, because I'm going to*, he said, pulling the boat out of the dock, *Strawberry Fields*. So we went *chop, chop, chop*, across the water, hair flying back, lots of spray in the face, feeling like you could jump from the seat. The banyan tree there in the harbor. Joe Petty, an island caretaker, who brought us his homemade coconut candy, his face withered like a dried fig. All the bags we bring to the dock and they take them in the car to the house, Almond Tree House. We all stop for a drink and watch the bloody tropical sky in sunset. They drink yellow birds in the harbor bar. We drink the ice. We get drunk a little bit. Eat popcorn.

Over in our big house called Almond Tree, Carrie makes crawfish. Carrie seems old and mean, maybe it's her small knuckle face, but the other cook, Muriel, got delirium tremens and talked about the little men in the kitchen. Carrie stands in the kitchen stuffing crawfish with her hands and when you go in the house, the tropical smell, soapy rotten fruit, hits, that smell again. In the main room, where we all lie on bamboo furniture given to us by the fabled Cousin Fred, who is a millionaire and lives in Miami, the side cabinets hold games, Scrabble, Blockhead, our favorite. When you open those doors, old cedar smell. Smell that again in a house you rent in Long Island, back, back, 1969, Bahamas.

We are barefoot all the busy day. The ocean is just a few blocks away on this island that spans three miles. You can go down there, follow the little sandy path with the tiny prickle balls that stick in your feet. You can gather jasmine that surrounds the beach, heavy and dense with sweetness, and marinate it in a jar with water and make perfume. Collect conch shells, big and pink like sunsets. Or, you can go back to the house and play in the garden with Mellie, the cook's son. Gather soldier crabs and sell them for fifty cents. Buy Cadbury chocolate at the Ruminette store, which is white and cloudy on the edges from the humidity. My legs are bony and brown, with scabs. Long and unkempt, my hair is bleached and silvery at the ends like ragged ribbons. John likes to fish, to gather the crabs, also. In the evenings we can't stop playing Blockhead, a silly game really, just a question of piling odd shapes on top of each other and getting the other person to screw up and collapse.

The family sits around in the living room. Uncles laughing, and Owen, seventeen, playing his incessant "Strawberry Fields" and "Baby You're a Rich Man" over and over, later years it's "My Sweet Lord." It plays all day long. The older one, Harrison, is usually fishing most days, darkened by the sun. We, my brother John and I, were digging in the dirt to catch soldier crabs with Mellie. Through the windows, I hear the music. There's an old shed there, worms, buckets, spider webs. Mellie and I fool around, take our clothes down. Harrison sees us, laughter at dinner. Face feeling red. No big deal. Friends come and go, in the living room, college friends, golf friends, Mom's boyfriends. I had to kiss this one guy on the cheek before going to bed, though I didn't want to, come on, he said.

We had Christmas here. We had a scraggly ocean pine, presents underneath. Carrie serves the crawfish in the shell, chunks melded with cream and a touch of sherry. Toasted on top. In the day, it's conch—conch chowder, cracked conch, conch fritters dipped in hot sauce. Years later I buy some conch from a Latin market in Manassas, Virginia, and they sit for days in their pearly shells in the refrigerator until they smell. Sometimes, we travel by boat to small out islands and catch grouper, build a fire, and grill it with lime juice. We all go to the Vic-hum at night, an outdoor club. Even the children. I wear Nancy's silver slides that are way too big and lip gloss and dance with the handsome English Cants, I am only ten, but I act eighteen.

I want to be like a combination of my aunt Moira, Uncle Harrison's wife, who is skinny, wears miniskirts, and has tortoise shell earrings, and my grandmother Nancy, who is glamorous. My mother is pretty but into the natural look, which I abhor. I raid Nancy's closet, wear her sandals, barely filling the front part. She says I have good legs. She wears bright pink lipstick, which I use. There's these dresses she wears, all bright colors, Lillies, she calls them, since they are designed by Lilly Pulitzer. They fight, her and Gene, my grandfather. Once he tossed out her clothes, out front on the main street. A man walked down below, it was late at night, and he drunkenly yelled: *O'Connor, bring out you womans*. Everyone knew what was going on in the island. One day threw her wigs out. He hid in the bathroom once in a fight, and she lit a fire under the door. We laugh, laugh, laugh about this at dinner, all of us. They drink a lot. Bourbon or pineapple rum. Yellow birds nightly.

When we go to the Vic-hum, with music and lights strung up, I usually go with the Cants. I hang out with BonBon, who's a little older, but I really like James, who's grown. All the men are brown from bonefishing and golf and then they wear pink shirts and you just see the whites of their eyes or their teeth. James dances with me a lot. Mom got pissed because I wear too much lip gloss. She's with this dark-eyed guy, Chris. They're dancing. She has dark kohled eyes. Beads. Dresses made from Indian bedspreads. You can get cracked conch here, too.

She smokes pot and it hurts me. I found a shoebox with a small carved pipe and a baggy of the stuff. You can die or go to jail for that stuff, teachers taught us, but they say, it's okay. Once they got some guy with an afro to talk me down at a party we were at because I was fretting. *It's no problem*, he said, *it's cool. I tried heroin and it was a drag. Pot's cool. Let your mom be*. Most of the time, she's out so we just play Blockhead, over and over.

Across from the house is the Ruminette, a store dark and smelly, sells candy and Bahamian white bread. There is a ghost white lady there who speaks with a duck accent. We get candy there or Piggly Wiggly, we buy Cadbury. Later on I buy Rothman cigarettes there, when I am seventeen. It opens with an old screen door, and we're always flopping through, buying some frippery for a nickel or two.

This is when Owen was normal, and everyone seemed to like each other. That all changed through the years, as voices silenced and clusters grew apart. The sound of that time was motor scooters outside, and the odd rooster crowing all day long, and the peppy Beatles somewhere on the breeze. Owen seemed to suddenly be quiet, his face changed, he was odd. He wanted to see my teeth once, kept telling me to open my mouth to see them, and it didn't seem right, it seemed scary, so I stopped, and there was more, once when everyone was out, he made me sit in a chair for two hours, not moving, and during that time he looked at me weird, and I thought I saw, out of the corner of my eye, him touching himself sometimes in his pants. I wasn't sure. When everyone came back, I was happy. I didn't say anything. What to say?

He used to laugh because he made me say over and over *The English Army had just won the war* from The Beatles and I couldn't, I kept flubbing it and laughing.

My grandfather gets stung by a stingray on the flats, bonefishing. I remember that, how he didn't cry. But it hurts like a mother, someone said. We were down at the Cant's Clinic. I sat in a chair. There was a blood spinning machine I kept looking at. There was a red part and a clear juice part and it was gross, we liked to say *eew, gross,* all the time. A girl came in whose ear had been bitten by a horse, it was see-through and dark red.

That night, it's the bar and yellow birds again for all of them, but we kids have to stay home, they say. BonBon, too. We ask if we can have drinks, and they say, sure, sure. So BonBon, my brother, and I all look up recipes in the bar book we find at home. All we can find are bee's knees, made of gin and honey, so we mix them up and all drink water glasses full of the stuff, and when they come back, they find the children drunken and throwing up. I remember sitting on the couch and leaning my head against BonBon's shoulder, everyone laughing.

We could go anywhere, do anything. Nobody cared. At home the maid yelled at us if we went to bed with dirty feet but here, we filled the bed with sand and slept in it. Baths drew too slow, anyway. And the water looked red. We swam and got sunburned and didn't know about sunscreen. There was Ban de Soleil, that's all, orange grease, good for tans.

Sometimes, I'd go with my grandparents for parties at the Island Golf club. Ladies wore pink, everyone wore pink. Always, brown people in pink. I remember ladies in my face, asking me things, polite answers. My grandmother wears nice jewelry. One thing, a big gold coin on a chain. My grandfather is too handsome. His hair is combed back and wet and smells like limes. He does real estate and foreign service, like being in the Far East and stuff, and then he does taxes in the garage and gets mad. There's a picture of him on the desk riding an elephant. They talk about Siam a lot in the fifties, and they knew the prince.

But they had hard times, too, they lost a baby in Siam and my grandmother says it lay in a pail outside the room. And the first baby was retarded and died at eight in an institution, so I'm not going to even pretend I know about pain next to them. And my younger uncle Owen was born and they couldn't revive him, so they stuck him with a huge needle in his heart, she said. And maybe that's why all of this now, she told me, this schizophrenia stuff. I haven't seen my uncle since he was nineteen, but he's now sixty. He lives in a old age home near us, because they take in mental patients, too. Thing is, medicines have made huge progress. He's doing quite well. He can't live with us, though, because maybe the medicine has squelched the illness, but his removal from society has made him an odd hothouse flower, a blank slate. His life experience halted and converted into a different atmosphere, that of the institution. In real life, he simply shuts down. We all had lunch in a restaurant once together and he was silent. He ate crab cakes. Then, he went back in. No one really said anything, I could hear that other laughter, light, polite laughter I know the sound of. It's a funny world I come from. Nobody cries, at funerals or anywhere, dry little conversations, handshakes, ham biscuits, bourbon. Things need to be pleasant. Things are not what they seem. Appearances are everything. We like how it looks to be pretty, to be tan. It's a world of niceness. When things are wrong, there is no language or ability, and we retreat off in our corners.

Is this what it's like to get old, now I'm thinking? All the foundations crumble until you're alone on the sand? Where's that house we stayed in, the one with the almond tree that dropped green fruit you could gnaw on, bitter and shreddy? And the Vic-hum, with the Christmas lights. All that Beatles music and the crawfish. Now that uncle is put away, maybe those were the best times for him, lying on the bamboo couch, listening to Paul McCartney, drinking Fresca. He played golf, he was the good one, the one who got the trophies. He only wore blue tropical shorts, and in those days, he didn't have that puffed, dull face he has now. He laughed. And the rest of us, all split up, my mother, pulled from the rest in strife and won't talk to them anymore and we stay in our own worlds and though I speak to my grandparents, all the weight of those heartbreaks from their kids pulls them down, visiting the younger uncle once a week, knowing he'll be alone when they go. Nobody else sees him. We're scared.

The last time I went there I was bursting with adolescence, seventeen, scouring for men, parties, fun. Michael Jackson blared from ramshackle cars that drove the sandy roads. Mellie was big, lustful, a man. We hung out in pool halls and smoked, *Thriller* playing in the background, flocks of teenagers from waspy states cluttered the tables on the perimeters, sucking down gin in underage abandon, adorned in Brooks Brothers and madras and headbands, like their parents. One particular khaki-clad boy, his hair brassy against his oily sun-reddened face, came up to me as I played pool.

"That's just not done," he said, and from this young man's voice came centuries of skewed learning. "You don't play with the help."

I was astonished, strangely ashamed, angered. I stood there and said nothing, had no words, but I felt ashamed because I knew I was out of the bounds of my own culture somehow,

Paprika
Melted butter
Chopped parsley

Cook lobster in boiling salted water until red. Remove from water and cool. Cut lobster in half lengthwise and remove meat from shell but save shell for stuffing. Heat milk in saucepan and set aside. Melt butter in small saucepan on low flame. Add onion and cook until tender. Add flour and grated cheese and stir continuously. Pour in hot milk and stir until mixture is thick and smooth. Add salt, pepper to taste, and sherry. Remove from heat. Cut lobster meat into small pieces--but not too finely. Add lobster to sauce and stuff into shell. Garnish with Parmesan, paprika, and melted butter. Place under broiler until golden brown. Garnish with parsley and serve.

❖ Joe Petty's Coconut Candy

½ cup water
2 cups grated coconut
1½ cups sugar
2 teaspoons vanilla extract
¼ teaspoon baking powder

Bring water to a boil in a saucepan. Add coconut and cook for 5 to 10 minutes. Add sugar. Cook for an additional 25 minutes until the coconut hardens, stirring constantly. Remove from heat and add vanilla and baking powder. Place waxed paper on cookie sheet. Drop coconut mixture by spoonfuls onto waxed paper and allow to cool and harden prior to serving.

❖ Yellow Birds

1 ounce light rum
¼ ounce Galliano
¼ ounce Crème de banane
2 ounces pineapple juice
2 ounces orange juice

Combine ingredients in a highball glass filled with ice and stir.

Chapter 3

Crednal

Glamour, 1972

The defining mood of the adults during my childhood was talk, incessant gabbing, sitting around on perched chairs on the lawn, talking of this and that. *What'll you drink, Nancy? Name your poison, my good man.*

And then, the shrine was approached, the elemental border between adulthood and childhood became that portioned spot, set with ice bucket, transparent bottles, different shaped glasses according to drinks: *highball, rocks, snifter*. Or, the complete martini ensemble: the shaker, the glasses whose neon silhouette on any restaurant sign comes to mean: *Come in, fun times. Ladies in short skirts selling cigarettes, gents in tuxedos, a real class act.*

The overwhelming conversational style was cynicism, irony with a touch of boredom thrown in. Laughter, downright hoots and snickers. Joking and mockery were always allowed. Sentimentalism, artifice were frowned upon. Perfection was a funny story with lots of imitative accents, that made the place crack with a wave of burst laughter from everyone, but especially her.

In those days, her laughter ruled the roost. This was her *domain*.

You *lived* for it.

Nancy, Nan. *Gaga*.

Because the real crime was to appear eager, unsophisticated. A boor. Or a bore, worse. Her favorite expression:

"What a bore." Said flatly, catapulting your dream of that subject sadly into oblivion. Forget that one.

"How gra-and!" meant you were in, did well.

"He's the utter end." Jettison that person into outer space.

"Listen here." You didn't want to hear *that* said, accompanied by a fixed finger in your face and snake coldness, a flood of angry words to follow. Somehow, you fucked up, and were snapped back in place. Harshly.

But, five seconds later, baby talk could follow, and you were in. For a while.

"Hey."

I looked up, she had called.

"Hey, listen."

"Yeah?"

I was busy, down in the cool "mudroom," with its subterranean dampness, shellacked brick floor, and big color TV, watching *Bewitched*. I was systematically devouring an entire box of Reese's Peanut Butter Cups, leaving a sea of fringed paper cups, like cicada shells.

"Come on up here, you."

To the upper realm, her room? Her lovely colonial palace (*real* colonial, mind you, not that artifice found in modern suburbia) was sharply divided in levels of status.

Mudroom, first level, children's area, next level, the kitchen and the maid owned that, I wasn't even allowed to look in. Up the stairs, one passed the "parlor," which every Virginian had to have. Untouchable, silvery satin loveseats, twin porcelain doggies by the fireplace, and best of all, Maggie, the china-faced delicate doll in a beaded dress I longed to play with, but was forbidden.

And then, winding up the stairs, past various rooms—the bedroom with the odd copper "bed warmer" that you filled with coals and slipped in between the covers, the rose wallpaper-covered bedroom I stayed in—was her domain:

The Master Bedroom, with ivory wall-to-wall carpeting (a mod extravagance in the sixties, now considered a white trash thing), a huge RCA TV on which I saw men walk on the moon, and her gargantuan bed, with its white cotton chenille bedspread with nubby balls all over it and twisty loops around the edges. A baby Siamese cat once strangled in those loops and we kept its sister, called, with originality, Kitty. The bed where she spent hour after hour propped up on pillows, fully clothed, over the covers, yellow manila pad in hand, writing all day long.

Sometimes, against her orders, I'd slip slowly up the stairs, a stair at a time, quiet as dust, sometimes caught by Bertha, the maid, but sometimes, sometimes, I'd make it, I'd slip in her room, her huge magnified eyes staring at me sternly, then smiling, like escaped sunlight.

But now, I was called forth, sent for.

Maybe she was writing something that reminded her of me. Sometimes, she'd let me look through her things, her closet or boxes which held little trinkets, from Thailand, the Far East, as she called it, which sounded exotic, and so long ago. Or I'd look at pictures. Her mother with her dark, suedey eyes and milk shoulders in dark lace. Or her, age five or six, seated at a tiny table serving tea in cups the size of rose petals, large starched ribbon in the golden hair. All alone, except for glass-eyed Maggie.

Or sometimes, she'd show me how she could pull off her thumb without bleeding, and we'd talk. She'd tell me how homely she was as a child (untrue!) and how she had to learn to be charming and social. That she decided, that's it, I'm alone here and how she had to be popular. When she danced with boys, she would say, *What a fine dancer you are!* or some such compliments, and they would line up to dance with her. She said I should try these things. I tried to shout them out to boys at dances, as we gyrated and shook to Bad Company and Aerosmith, but they couldn't hear what I said, *what? What?* so I gave up, and did what everyone else did, smoked in the back, drank beers, cruised in cars to Pizza Hut. It was a different era.

Her Rules:

Never say "drapes." We say "curtains."

Never say "silverware." Say "silver."

When something is awful, she'd say "cheesy." She ripped many superfluous bows off of my dresses because they were "cheesy," and one such bow actually was a Cheddar cheese color, which got me to thinking for years to come.

Never say "wealthy." It's "rich."

She definitely didn't eat. She was thin. She smoked. And she drank, two drinks made by Gene, after five o'clock, up in the ivory carpeted bedroom, while they watched *Agronsky and Company.*

We were poor, which to my mother meant "cool," having grown up rich, and now, rejecting it, she was artistic, hip, intellectual. My mother bought me Mexican blouses, one at a time, and we would handwash them and hang them outside to dry. Then we'd iron their stiffness until perfect, crisp. And wear them until ragged and used.

Nancy bought lovely sorbet-toned turtlenecks from the shop in town, the super expensive one that sold Kenneth Jay Lane jewelry and flats with gold buckles. She bought them in identical styles, ten at a time, in a flurry of colors.

Or, she'd order from catalogues, Gorkies, L.L.Bean, Talbots, duplicates of everything.

I'd play her sometimes, circling from catalogues what I wanted, a pique tennis dress, the perfect pool cover-up, perfect for lounging around in at our incense-reeking, scrappy pool-less backyard.

I wanted glamour so damn badly. I hungered for it, smeared my face with toxic oil pastels for makeup, played with Barbie in my window box for days, her cool New York penthouse that she redesigned hourly.

I received a pale yellow, quilted nylon bathrobe for my birthday once, and wore it nightly to dinner, impeccably, with my hair pushed up in a severe bun. It was the one perfect, spotless thing I owned, that existed in a house of Indian bedspreads on the stone walls, a giant tree trunk as a table, floors that gave three-inch splinters at every slide.

Gaga let me wear her long Pucci gowns, which fell in crumpled folds around my ankles. And she even let me wear her jewels, I won't even get into her jewels, her walnut-size black star sapphire.

She gave me some diamond rings, and a prized sapphire birthstone ring that I lost swimming in the creek, and was too heartbroken to tell anybody.

Oh, and makeup. I used to beg my mother to wear makeup, envisioning a Barbara Eden sort of look, smooth background of seamless pale blue on lids, with a nice sharp black line like a tadpole against the lid, flipping up its tail at the end. And then, lashes. Fakes! I longed for them.

Mother wouldn't have it. Bonne Bell gloss, at the most, maybe mascara.

She would, however, set her brown, glossy hair in orange juice cans for hours as she primped for John, my future stepfather, to come over.

Gaga went to Mr. Alfredo, and I got to go also. She drove in her big boat of a car, sailing along at eighty miles an hour in a pale air-conditioned velveteen oasis of Muzak and her occasional conversation. My knees had grown hard from scrabbling around finding lost pencils on the hard, screw-covered industrial floor of our Jeep, and, shivering as cold air always leaked in. I sat back and melted in comfort.

Finally, we would arrive at Mr. Alfredo's lair. He would scream with delight when she entered, rushing, comb in hand to kiss kiss kiss her face in a flurry and he always made the appropriate fuss over me, although Gaga was the star.

And I'd watch, in awe, as he pulled lick after lick of hair through that white baldy cap and smother it with blue stuff that turned a frothy gray and smelled like ammonia, and then she sat back covered in a tent and got it washed out. She looked weird that way, vulnerable, like a little animal.

And then, stage two, rolled in curlers, blue prickly ones in neat rows with little yellow ones around the edges and she's then stuck under the loud dryer for hours. Not once did she get a manicure. Not once. She kept her nails undone, no polish, and wore an old ring with a dome of diamonds.

And only a smear of lipstick, "Shocking Pink" as it was called, Revlon, I remember. Bright, bright neon pink against her leathery, tanned skin and the tiger-striped, shiny helmet that emerged from Mr. Alfredo's gleaming, teased and high, but not too much. Smelling like Diorissimo, wearing Lilly Pulitzer summer dresses with aplomb, with white leather thongs, and those goddamn legs, still going strong now at ninety-five.

Her little toy poodles, Violet and Primrose, would jump with joy when she got out of the car, leaving faint white marks on her shins, against the tan, from their claws.

She'd scratch their tiny furry skulls and they'd settle down. Gene would brush her cheek, admire her hair, approach the bar, pour with a little aluminum jigger the proper amount of bourbon. I'd have a coke.

There may have been those smoky, powdery almonds they loved.

Once they brought us all up to New York for the weekend and we stayed at The Waldorf. It was fancy and large, and I was highly impressed. We entered the room with our bags and immediately Gene ordered drinks brought to the room. They came with a small silver bowl full of those smoked nuts.

They clicked on the news. They were news junkies.

They lay on the white bed, in their clothes, both sets of eyes magnified like bugs, and stared as Nixon spoke, and I lay on the floor, the carpet making the bottoms of my elbows marred and bumpy.

❖ **Nancy's Baked Apricot Chicken**

    One 4-ounce package Lipton Onion Soup Mix
    One 3½-pound chicken, cut up
    1 bottle Russian dressing
    1 jar apricot preserves

Sprinkle onion soup mix in baking dish. Arrange chicken pieces on top. Pour Russian dressing over chicken. Spread apricot preserves on top. Bake chicken at 350°F for 1 hour and 30 minutes, basting occasionally.

Chapter 4

Virginia Revisited

The Seventies

My parents divorced when I was four. We then moved to Georgetown in D.C., where assorted bohemian types passed through the house. There was Gene, a black man with a short trimmed afro, always impeccably dressed in an old-fashioned way, given that everyone else, including my mother, wore the beads and bells of the hippie uniform, but most surprising because he had no home. A quiet man, who would suddenly shake in uncontrollable laughter. I probably owe my first love of painting because of Gene. He always had an easel set up in Dupont Circle, and he was always immaculate in a suit, raincoat, proper shoes, while around him cavorted bongo-players, long-hairs, druggies. I think he crashed at our house a few times. He let me play with his paints.

Then, Hank came on the scene, my mother's boyfriend, a photographer. He would run all the way down the stairs of our townhouse in Georgetown with photo paper in hand to process in the light, usually of his body. He taught us the proper technique for bacon, which was hardly novel, but we didn't know how to cook anything then, so we studied his every flick of the fork and turn to perfect our favorite food at the time. My mother worked and we were left with "maids" as we called them. The first one was fine, named Rosie, who wore a wig and kept her false teeth in a jar by the bed. But the next one was strangely cruel. Martha was a large woman, and favored my brother. She would coddle him, while instructing me to pick up lint off the floor. One day she sent me across the busy intersection (I was five) to get a Twinkie and an RC cola for her, but when I finally somehow maneuvered all that, the bag had softened with condensation and the cola fell on the step, smashing to pieces. After her rage, I told my mother everything, who fired her promptly and had a celebration party. I don't know who came next, but I know I hated my school. Kids would tease me. I've always felt outside of the crowd, a social misfit, my whole life. Given a small amount of money for lunch and the bus that I took everyday, I decided one morning to stay on the bus and skip school.

I remember the day well. I bought candy. I visited a museum. When I walked in they looked at me oddly and asked me if I wanted to go to the "lavatory." Not knowing what the hell they meant, I said yes, and found myself frustratingly in a toilet. I somehow got over to Dumbarton Oaks, a park. I asked a lady with a young son to tell me the time, so I could get home on time, but she forgot, and finally, I decided to walk home.

Apparently, my mother had worried when I didn't arrive home, and then panicked when she called the school and they said I had never even attended. When I walked back down the brick street to our house, a policeman was holding my crying mother, and they both looked up in shock as I walked up. That promptly ended my life in Washington, D.C. It was then my grandparents fixed up the small cottage on their estate, Crednal, and we moved to Virginia.

Don't get any other ideas in your head: Virginia is the South. The main sustenance of my childhood was southern food, and I don't mean white-trash southern cooking, with marshmallows and cans of mushroom soup, I mean food that has survived the Civil War, the same things my great-grandparents ate, and all of their relatives as well.

Namely, ham. Soaked for days, simmered, cooked, salty and chewy like an old strip of leather, it would sit covered in wax paper in the "cold room" or the pantry and find its way into ham rolls usually, the quintessential southern delight. Most people actually refer to them as ham biscuits, and yes, this is typical, especially "beaten biscuits," which are made of a dough that needs considerable pounding for hours. Why I don't know, because these things are dry, tasteless wafers which crumble as soon as bitten into. And biscuits aren't much better, crumbly, half the thing falls to the floor. Our preference was the risen yeast roll with a bit of sugar in the mix. It was common to see these treasures lined up like tiny pillows on old blackened pans, covered in damp dishtowels surrounding the old woodstove in the kitchen, whose heat would help them develop.

After they baked, they would be stuffed with butter and a few thin slivers of the ham. Then they would sit on a pan and get reheated later, until crusty, dribbling with butter, a soft crunchy taste with the salty ham. Heaven.

I mentioned Bertha earlier and she knew how to cook. Bertha's tomatoes are a fixture at special dinners, though outsiders don't get them. Tomatoes cooked for hours with bacon grease, celery, onions, brown sugar. They tend to be too sweet for most people, almost a gluey marmalade. Then there is the ubiquitous chicken salad, which my grandmother Nancy remembers as a child. They would chase the chicken, wring its neck, pluck it, boil it for hours because it was tough as nails, chop every morsel of meat (unlike today, where it's only breast meat), make homemade mayonnaise, and toss with celery and onion. No wedding or summer supper was complete without this, though how commonplace it has become, with every deli and diner supplying a mushy, chopped version. But the true version was silky and delicate. And iced tea, Bertha's tea: brewed strong and mixed with mint, orange and lemon juices, sugar syrup. We drank this in tall silver goblets.

Most days I ate Vienna sausages, however. Bertha didn't let us poke around the kitchen. Out of sheer frustration with my whiny insistence, she would give me some tuna salad with relish and saltines. These days were long and boring, but with my uncle around, John and I had fun. We'd listen to his records and generally annoy him. I collected dried husks of cicadas by the old trees and crushed them or played with them. We went down to the pond with our bamboo poles and worms as the mist rose, and the locusts screeched, and pulled in tens of bluegills, one after another. We'd even fillet those tiny fish and drench them in flour and fry them. On Sundays, we'd all go over to the large mansion called Welbourne across the street, a well-known fixture in the Civil War, and play stickball. All the young people in the area went there, to mingle, drink beer, hit tennis balls with old broomsticks on the large expansive lawn into the dirt road. My mother, my uncles, and us, my brother and I, we went and played all Sunday.

It was there that my mother saw my future stepfather John

Daniel, a young sculptor, coming back home after attending Pratt in Brooklyn. It was instant, she said, an immediate knowledge we all long for.

After that, it was a short time until they were married. John was a kind man, quiet, an intensely talented sculptor whose work was scattered over his whole yard, abstract forms cast in aluminum and steel. He grew up in Delaplane, Virginia, but had studied in New York and traveled and now, he was back, back to the old world of mosquitoes and ham biscuits, iced tea and slow conversation. He met Ann, and they married. They are still together, deeply connected. John Daniel is a rare sort, a true gentleman of honor in the old southern way, and yet, a man who works with steel in his studio to awkward, screechy jazz.

The wedding was an odd animal—a combination of old Virginia and the hippiness they embodied. They were into kayaks, so the party took place at Crednal, the large estate where we lived next to the pond. There were the old ham rolls, and all the good old-fashioned stuff, yet John Daniel and his friends decided to go kayaking naked in front of everyone. Old Virginians stood around in Brooks Brothers drinking gin watching a bunch of guys—John Daniel's old cronies from UVA—splash around naked, while Bertha passed another warm ham roll. My mother with her long hair and bangs in a Mexican embroidered dress and no one said a thing. Everyone was very polite.

We moved. John Daniel had a large farm in Delaplane. There was a tenant farmer in an old stone house and they moved, and John started to rebuild it for us to live in. In the meantime, my brother and I stayed with his parents, Elsie and Jack. Jack had been a solid man, proudly known in the community, but now the poor guy had gone senile. He did weird things, like pee in the silver drawer. My brother and I simply observed. It was all new and odd. He would sit for hours in his recliner chair, and we'd politely sit there, watching Mutual of Omaha's *Wild Kingdom*. Elsie, or Tuttie as she liked us to call her, was sweet, with the most lilting accent from Petersburg. She called us "chillen." And she was an incredible cook.

We started going to church on Sundays, with a big family supper afterward. Life became a little subdued, dampened. Gone were the wild toasts flung into the fireplace, or the weird uncle or my grandmother lying in her boudoir. They weren't the eccentric grandparents I knew from my father's side either, no curried bananas or altars in the home or homemade perfume. It was actually terribly dull. Tuttie always wore a dress and stockings, even gardening. We'd wash up and go to church, a church like all churches with that horrible sour smell in the rectory and the insufferable boredom and the endless discussion of sinning. Then we'd all come back to Tuttie's and have the supper—and what a supper. Ham, of course. "Roast of beef" as she called it, with gravy. Mashed potatoes. Squash casserole. Homemade bread-and-butter pickles Tuttie had made. And her crowning glory, her damson pie, which is unlike anything you've ever had. Damson plum preserves are whipped with egg, sugar, a tad of cornmeal, and mixed with egg whites. The result is dense and pudding-like, sour and sweet at the same time.

I think at this point I was slowly falling apart in the most private way, which was how it was done. My mother and John Daniel were deeply in love and kind of lost in their own little world, living up at the house, rebuilding it lovingly. I was torn away from my Nancy and Gene, whom I adored, and yet I was relieved to be away from Owen, who creeped me out. I didn't have a home, I was staying with Tuttie in her old-fashioned house, and I felt desperate and trapped. Unbeknownst to anyone, I stole from the drugstore. I don't know why, I just shoplifted. I stole haircurlers, makeup, anything, condoms. There was no reasoning to the practice, but it was regular and exciting. I packed a small bag and kept it in the closet, because I had a new plan that I would run away in the early dawn by hitch hiking out on 66. You could hear the trucks barreling by, and that reminded me daily of my quest. I just wanted to get out. I never did it then, though. It took me about five years to finally leave, when I boarded at a nearby school. But, the fantasy of running away one early dawn was a strange solace that kept me going.

Then the house was ready and we moved up there, and although it was a pretty cottage, set in the tranquility of three hundred or so acres, with a big garden, for me, a new teenager, it was death. There was nothing to do: we had one black-and-white TV 12-inch, which was in my mother's room. You couldn't sit on her bed, so you sat on the floor and watched. Most of the channels were fuzzy, and we watched *Masterpiece Theater* most times anyway.

Or food: at this point, I wanted bright, crisp artificial snacks. My mother's pantry had none of these, you would open it to find antique Mason jars of brown rice or whole wheat flour. In the refrigerator would be a hunk of Reggiano Parmesan, some local eggs still with tiny feathers stuck to them, unpasteurized milk with a huge layer of yellow fat on top—as a teenager, I was horrified. At this point I befriended a girl at school who came from a large Sicilian family of ten girls, all spaciously living in a house of modern comforts, thick shag carpets, a refrigerator crammed with soft drinks and Cheez Whiz, loud stereos in every room, a bug zapper, giant TVs, Camaros parked in clusters on the lawn, around a giant pool, and easy access to the town of Leesburg, which to me was a huge metropolis. Her name was Nono, which is ninth in Italian, her order in the group. She lived in a world of fantasy and my only escape was to go to her house. They had parties around the big pool and teenagers were abounding at all times. She called my house "the Shanty."

I was so frustrated. I remember being grounded for this and that and the burning frustration and anger of living there. For many people, it would have been heaven. For my parents, I think it was. They were just vastly unaware of who I was at that time, and teenagers, after all, need to fume and argue at times. We have always been diametrically opposite. I craved the city, activity, artificiality, people. They disdained the suburbs, malls, frozen food, they were Luddites. I spent my hours of frustration in my small room, angry, hot (no air conditioning, which I am sensitive about now, I can't live without it), writing poems in my room. Sometimes I'd play around in the kitchen and cook things—funny how these are the two things I ended up doing in my life, cooking and writing. When I began high school, I was sent to the local girl's boarding school. I was a day student at first, but as soon as I could, I boarded, and finally, I was free from Greenwood. Even now, I feel a constriction across my chest as I think of living there. Looking back, it is the food that stays and I am grateful for. Forget all that boredom and anger, that is in the past. We ate very well, better than anyone. I can see that now. We were odd adventurers, while the majority of the people we knew ate canned chicken soup casseroles, turkey on white bread, Hamburger Helper. I know, because when I went to their houses, I was shocked. *Is this their dinner?* You have to understand the extreme diligence and care my mother and John gave to meals: most of the vegetables would be just-picked and organic from their garden, cooked by my mother, who seemed as if she had been trained by the Cordon Bleu. Coming from the Queen of Apricot Chicken, I have no clue where she picked it up. All those years of experimenting with cannelloni and granola, and she finally had gelled into an artist. They gathered wild mushrooms, made their own wine, shot their own deer and butchered it on the kitchen island, drove three hours down south to procure the best free-range chickens and rabbits, tracked down only the finest cheeses available, hunks of Reggiano, weeping balls of buffalo mozzarella, greenest olive oil, eggs with yolks like small apricots. And they were ahead of their time, this was the seventies, long before Alice Waters. They were riding the wave of the hippie movement, which had faded from the war activism and free love of the sixties into a grand movement of living off the land in the seventies. We had friends in communes, hairy-legged woman and bearded, long-haired men would invite us to meals of unappetizing bowls of hummus and brown casseroles, hodgepodges of the "health movement." Banjos would play, or Irish tinwhistles or a stereo would wail with Dylan's whiny ballads. It was here I tried marijuana, with their children one day up in a bedroom where we found a stash, to my utter disappointment. They would have goat roasts, and lead walks across the land wearing caftans.

But the nexus of all the new influence on food was the new organic garden model, started by a couple from Vermont:

Helen and Scott Nearing. By the time we knew them, they had moved to Maine. According to their Web site, "In 1932, at the height of the Great Depression, Helen and Scott Nearing moved from their small apartment in New York City to a dilapidated farmhouse on 65 acres in Vermont. For over 20 years, they created fertile, organic gardens, hand-crafted stone buildings, and a practice of living simply and sustainably on the land. In 1952, they moved to the Maine coast, where they later built their last stone home."

We had seen, on a recent long and sweaty car trip to Maine, with a stunned and reverent awe, their amazing Maine garden and that pretty much became the standard at Greenwood. Scott Nearing had single-handedly cleared the land of every single rock with his wheelbarrow, dragged huge bundles of seaweed from the ocean to cure as fertilizer. Their garden had paths and gates and riotous beds of unimaginable vegetables for the seventies—we hadn't seen baby striped eggplant, fresh basil (especially ten varieties—Thai basil, purple basil, lemon basil, Genoa basil, etc.). No one knew of tiny yellow pear-shaped tomatoes! Or the tiniest fingerling potatoes, just dug from the earth, so sweet and feathery light. Ann and John Daniel were seeking gourmands: unknown and silent leaders of the new American food movement, and I was a happy recipient of their experiments. Certain seventies items that we consumed along the way:

QUICHE

They were starved for new tastes, John and Ann. They were the new Americans, the mavericks, but a decade ahead of everyone. By now they had abandoned the granola and the heavy, dense home-baked bread. They were delving into quiche long before every café placed a slice on their hackneyed brunch menu, accompanied by an artfully twisted slice of orange. My mother made delicately fluffy quiches with local bacon, bright yellow from organic eggs. We would occasionally visit my real father, Mark, who had remarried and lived back at Francis and Mary's farm. This would be a bit of a culinary risk if he was cooking. One never knew what might end up on the plate on these nights. One had to admire his bold creativity, his flair for the unusual, but unfortunately, it didn't always gel: turkey liver stew has become legendary for its unsavoriness. On the other hand, he doesn't bore with his cooking. He has a streak of the innovater, the genius. He is the Ferran Adriá (creator of the bizarre and different restaurant, El Bulli, in Barcelona) of our family, sometimes odd and off mark, but sometimes creating a surprisingly new flavor. He also loves condiments, I noticed. He'll have a lazy Susan with endless varietals of hot sauce, chutneys, salsas, etc. for dabbing on his lunch. I think he is a man of variety, a man who likes the complex and the wild. It is quiche that seemed to mark this decade: my father's second marriage did not work out. A few years later, he married Virginia North, a young and pretty Englishwoman, with long golden hair and bright red lips. She was eccentric and artistic like himself, with a great interest in bugs. Their wedding feast consisted of a delicious repaste of heavy, dense quiches, served on the same grassy lawn I mentioned in the beginning of this book.

PESTO

We discovered pesto in a blind fury of desire. Once you taste real pesto, freshly ground with biting garlic, the burst of flavor sandblasts the years of Chef Boyardee into oblivion. By now, pesto is just so old hat—so Ruby Tuesday, so Costco, because once again it has been made "lite." But try it again: use a mortar and pestle, handfuls of freshly picked Genoan basil leaves, real garlic, green olive oil, Reggiano Parmesan, pine nuts. Keep it rough and dense and then toss it on whole wheat shells and eat it at room temperature. Or cold, from a large earthenware bowl like we did. Eat it before the bright grassiness fades. I read once a trick to keep the green and it does work: add one spoonful of yogurt to the mix. Eat it with your hands directly from the bowl, ravenously, or on a road trip like we did going to Maine. Each little shell will scoop some pesto up and burst in your mouth.

Around this time, John Daniel went to Utica, New York, to participate in a welding project for sculptors. Utica is blue collar, rough, and very Italian. Because of this trip, he discovered pesto, cannoli, and fresh mozzarella, bringing it back to us like a merchant coming from the Silk Road with bags of jewels. We tore through these delights and, like addicts, demanded more: on trips to Maine we had to stop and buy big boxes tied in string of cannoli, and endless lumps of mozzarella to eat with our Virginia tomatoes (if they could survive the journey without us hunking off slice after slice).

FONDUE

Yes, we bought the avocado-hued pot, the chafing candles, the long forks. We savored the melted cheeses, the boiling oil for the bourguignonne, even the chocolate. We moved on quickly, though, to other more erudite versions of the hot pot, influenced by a family Japanese friend: shabu-shabu. Many an evening was spent around a boiling pot, swishing paper-thin slices of beef and drenching them in sauce. I remember my mother ordering the beef from the old-time butcher in Middleburg, who has since moved on. And we have a terrible family fondue story: The Macmaniss event. We, Ann and John, my brother John and I, were invited to a fondue party in the suburbs of Washington, where we descended like a small pack of starved wolflings. A huge fondue display decorated their shag-carpeted living room and we attacked. They had all the fondues, and we sampled and gorged for hours. Just when I had basically cleared out the fondue table single-handedly, scrounging down every last hunk of French bread and sliver of raw meat, I noticed my hovering brother had disappeared. This was an emergency situation. There was still good fondue to devour, and yet he was gone. At this point, by certain rough and offhand comments flung by adults drifting into the dining room, I started to realize a "situation" had occurred. This was immediately evident because of my years of training in this family, when questions were never asked, but one had to home in instantly on the subtle shifts in emotional environment for the sake of survival. An imperceptible flurry was developing around the staircase, yes, in fact a line had gathered outside the bathroom. With John gone, and the telltale long line, I knew: My brother had an "attack." We all seem to have some form of a sensitive stomach, prone to "attacks." Perhaps fondue was not the best choice. I located my parents and we all stampeded up the shagged stairs to save John. "Some kid is in there" an irate man warned us, and then, when they finally got him to unleash the boarded door, to their horror, the worst had happened. My poor brother had inadvertently slaughtered the entire white shag bathroom. What could one do? Everything was blasted. Beyond repair with paper towels. it required total renovation. Sandblasting, caulking, and general fumigation. What we did next was the worst thing. We banded as a team: my parents went to get the car. John and I stayed in the bathroom. We waited the allotted time, and then tore down the stairs, out the front door, never to appear again. We should have called, pulled aside the hostess. But how? Our words fizzled on the air of horror. We shirked. Fondue faded.

Like everything in this family, simple communication may have somehow brought us to a better place, but we always seemed unable to deal with even the tiniest amount of shame or struggle, preferring to completely retreat in our separate corners. Needless to say, we never heard from them again.

MUSHROOMS

Welcome to the obsession of John and Ann for the present. They will spend days trekking the woods of Virginia, Maine, wherever they can, foraging for every mushroom imaginable. They come back with sacks of morels, piles of buttery chanterelles, puffballs, oyster mushrooms, chicken-of-the-woods. They dry them in drying racks, they sauté them in butter. They even grow shiitakes in logs with shiitake plugs. Occasionally, they order a truffle for a new flavor, shaved over hot polenta and cold mascarpone, their favorite style.

HAM

Through the trends, however, the old favorites remain, icons of history and culture. If one food has lasted, one representative of the then and now, it would be our beloved dry, husky ham. I suppose pork has some hidden power other meats don't contain: what other meat is forbidden in several world religions? What meat can possible evoke more nostalgia and love than pork's many manifestations, from pit-cooked barbecue, hot dogs, bacon, or the world of varieties found in the foods of Asia,

Italy, or Eastern Europe? A ham has a presence, somehow, reigning supreme on an Easter dinner table. It is from John Daniel I've learned the arduous preparation of a Virginia ham. His father smoked his own, and they hung out in a separate smokehouse out back, covered in pepper and spots of green mold. John soaks the ham overnight and scrubs it. Then he simmers it in an old oblong pan his father used for his purpose. Next, he stamps it all over with pepper thumbprints and than bakes it slowly for two hours. Lastly, he uses his sharp, old steel knives to slice it paper thin.

I was called by an old Virginian family to cater their father's funeral the other day. The son said, *I heard you do it right, the old-fashioned way.* The mother said, when I talked to her, *I don't know what we want. Just not real fancy. You know. Country.* I actually knew exactly. What joy for me to make this food. I thought of the man while I cooked his food, with a certain somber care: this is for you, man. This will celebrate who you were. I made exactly the same thing everyone has been eating for generations: when the bedraggled boys arrived home from the Civil War, torn and bleeding, the women boiled the ham. They rolled the biscuits. They chased down the chicken. I made ham rolls, chicken salad tea sandwiches, pound cake. I made sweet ice tea, and lemonade.

The darkly clad group trickled in from the church to the parish hall, gingerly, not sure of what to say or how to approach the widow. But then, they saw the food, and settled down. They were in the kitchen of their grandmother, by the woodstove. Some men I knew from various battered Virginia families stood guard by the table in their crumpled suits, waiting for the next delivery of warm ham rolls. Their soft sighs of delight, their gasps were of delight—that still, comfort is this simple.

❖ Virginia Ham and Yeast Rolls

Bake the rolls (recipe follows). Slice Virginia ham into paper-thin slices. It will be crumbly at times, and stringy, but that's okay. Make sure some slices have a bit of fat as well, for flavor. Slice the rolls open horizontally and on each place a pat of butter and a slice of ham and put on a baking sheet in rows. Bake at 350°F for 15 to 20 minutes until golden and hot.

❖ Yeast Rolls

> One .25-ounce package quick-rising active dry yeast
> ¾ cup warm water (105° to 115°F)
> 2 tablespoons sugar
> 2 tablespoons vegetable oil
> ½ teaspoon salt
> 1 large egg
> 2½ to 2¾ cups all-purpose flour
> Butter, softened for brushing

Dissolve yeast in water in a large bowl. Add sugar, oil, salt, and egg. Stir to dissolve sugar and salt. Stir in 1 cup of the flour until smooth. Turn oven on low for about a minute to warm, then turn it off. Cover bowl with cloth and place on rack over bowl of hot water in the oven. Let rise for 15 minutes. Grease 9-inch square pan. Stir down batter and add 1½ cups flour. Stir until mixed, 3 minutes. If sticky, knead in another ¼ cup flour. Divide dough into sixteen balls. Cover with cloth and place on rack over bowl of hot water for 25 minutes. Heat oven to 425°F. Bake for 12 to 15 minutes. Brush tops with butter and serve warm.

❧ Bertha's Tomatoes

1 cup diced onions
1 cup diced celery
½ cup bacon fat
Four 14.5 ounce cans tomatoes, coarsely chopped (into
    quarters)
½ cup sugar
Salt and pepper to taste

In large saucepan or a saucepot, slowly sauté onions and celery in bacon fat until translucent. Add rest of ingredients and cook slowly for 3 hours, or until thick, dark, and caramelized

❧ Tuttie's Squash Casserole

2 pounds yellow squash, cut into ¾-inch slices
1 cup chopped onion
1 teaspoon salt
¼ teaspoon black pepper, or to taste
4 tablespoons (½ stick) butter, plus some for greasing
1 cup crumbled saltine crackers
½ cup milk
1 egg, beaten
1 cup shredded cheddar cheese
Buttered bread crumbs

Put the squash, onion, salt, and pepper in a large saucepan. Add a small amount of water. Cover and cook the squash until tender, stirring occasionally and adding more water if necessary. Drain and stir in the butter.

Butter 1½-quart baking dish well. Stir crackers into squash mixture, and turn into the baking dish. Pour milk and egg over squash, sprinkle with the cheese, and stir. Top with bread crumbs. Bake uncovered at 350°F for 20 minutes, until milk is absorbed and squash casserole is bubbly. Serve hot. Serves 4 to 6.

❖ Damson Pie

½ pound (2 sticks) butter or margarine*
1 cup sugar
5 eggs, separated
1 cup damson preserves or jelly*
2 tablespoons cornmeal
1 teaspoon vanilla extract
2 unbaked pie shells

Cream butter or margarine and sugar until fluffy. Add the egg yolks, and beat well. Add preserves, cornmeal, and vanilla. Beat egg whites until stiff but not dry, fold into preserve mixture and divide between pie shells. Bake at 350° or 375°F† for about 35 minutes. Be careful that the pies do not get too brown.

From a book of favorite recipes compiled by the members and friends of the Episcopal Church of Leeds Parish. Markham, Virginia. August 2, 1992. 150th anniversary.

❖ Cannelloni

1 tablespoon olive oil
1 tablespoon butter
½ cup chopped onion
1 teaspoon minced garlic
¼ cup chopped parsley

---

* I believe Tuttie switched to margarine in her last years and I think damson jelly was an alternative when she didn't have preserves.
† The thermometer on her stove was completely erratic.

1 pound lean ground beef
½ cup finely diced mortadella
¼ cup grated Parmesan cheese
2 eggs
1 teaspoon dried oregano
½ teaspoon salt
¼ teaspoon black pepper
12 crêpes
1 cup marinara sauce (recipe follows)
2 cups béchamel sauce (recipe follows)

Preheat oven to 350°F.

Heat the olive oil and butter in a sauté pan. Add onion, garlic, and parsley and cook over medium heat for 3 to 5 minutes. Do not brown. Add ground beef, stir until browned, and add the mortadella. Sauté for a few minutes. Chop in a processor to a paste. Add 2 tablespoons of the Parmesan, the eggs, oregano, and salt and pepper.

Divide filling among crêpes. Roll to enclose filling.

Spread some marinara sauce over the bottom of a baking dish. Arrange the cannelloni in dish. Spoon the béchamel sauce and remaining marinara sauce over the top. Sprinkle with the remaining 2 tablespoons of Parmesan.

Bake for 20 to 25 minutes, until brown.

❖ Marinara Sauce

2 tablespoons olive oil
3 cloves garlic, minced
1 medium yellow or white onion
Salt and black pepper
1 teaspoon dried oregano
1 tablespoon fresh chopped basil or 1 teaspoon dried basil
Two 28-ounce cans tomatoes (whole, peeled, or crushed with
    their juice) or 2 pounds fresh tomatoes

3 tablespoons tomato paste
1 whole bay leaf

Heat olive oil in large skillet over medium heat for about 1 minute, then add half the garlic. When the garlic starts to brown, add the onion and stir. Let the onion cook for about a minute, stirring frequently, then add salt and pepper to taste remaining garlic, oregano, and basil. Stir well. Continue to cook for about 5 minutes, until the onion is soft and translucent. Do not brown.

Add the tomatoes with juice, tomato paste, and bay leaf. Stir and bring sauce to a slow boil, then turn down the heat and let it simmer uncovered for at least 1 hour, until sauce is thick. When it is done, emulsify and thicken it with a handheld blender.

❖ Béchamel Sauce

2 tablespoons butter
2 tablespoons flour
1¼ cups hot milk
Salt and white pepper

Melt the butter in a heavy-bottomed saucepan. Stir in the flour and cook for about 2 minutes, stirring constantly, until the paste cooks and bubbles a bit. Don't let it brown.

Add the hot milk, continuing to stir as the sauce thickens. Bring to a boil. Add salt and pepper to taste, lower the heat, and cook, stirring, for 2 to 3 minutes more.

Remove from the heat.

Chapter 5

Maine

Sea Urchins and Blueberry Pie, 1982

Afterthe year was spent in Virginia, with a Christmas foray to the Bahamas, we tended to summer
in Maine, due to the cool weather. The problem with Maine is
getting there. It's a long, arduous journey and we all have our
different styles of maneuvering it. My brother plows through,
pulling over to sleep in the car when he can't take it. That's
usually at three in the morning somewhere near Hartford.
Being a humorous man, he morphs into a Mainer personality
somewhere around Hartford. Call him up on a cell phone for a
progress report and you've located an eighty-year-old lobster
fisherman from Deer Isle: *uh yep, passed the shipyahd heeyah,
wicked good, well past Hahtfohd now.* He pretty much stays in
that character the whole time in Maine. I've forgotten to mention he's a consummate actor, occasionally starring in local
shows.

• • •

Gene and Nancy always did the same expedient method of travel, and they'd never tell you *when*. It was a mysterious ritual they kept to themselves. When are you going up? Oh, I don't know. Maybe next week. Then, a day later, they'd call you from Maine. They suddenly went without warning. They accepted no frills or pampering on that trip. Their Volvo packed to the brim with golf clubs and tomatoes, the frisky toy poodles Violet and Primrose, always a box of Wheat Thins, and always the dreaded small plastic yellow bucket, which I'm sure you can guess its purpose. We've always laughed about the bucket, apparently they didn't even want to lose a mere second on the trek, and yet, they always stopped in New Hampshire at the border to shop the huge liquor supermarkets, where you saved five cents by buying the industrial-size gin and bourbon bottles. And how difficult must it be to maneuver that bucket in a cramped Volvo with a dog, at eighty years old? When a rest stop could be a mere five-minute blip? One cannot say. I've no doubt divulged too much.

My method of driving up is nil, since I can't do it. I have a terrible phobia of highways, especially trucks. For a while, I could only take the small roads around Virginia to drive to D.C., taking me hours to get there. Now, I've trained myself with beta blockers to forgo all that. I can spin down 495 no problem, the old bottle of beta blockers in the glove compartment as some faint memory of my fragility, a security blanket type of thing. But I can't do Maine. I can't wile around those circuitous strips of roads around Manhattan as every cantankerous seafood purveyor barrels by at eighty miles an hour. I can't handle the clutch of Mack trucks swinging by the Hartford beltway. So I am always escorted somehow, by my friends, or family, like an old Tennessee Williams character.

Ann and John Daniel take the ultra scenic route, designed for dogs. They wind their way through every coal mining town, every tiny easeway, stopping at preferred dog-friendly rest stops and hotels. They drive along roads at thirty miles an hour, three hours off the main trek, to find some small diner from years back. Or they'll maddeningly pause for an hour or two for a mosquito-plagued forage for mushrooms off the side of a small road. They pack up a large picnic as well, agush with assorted favored snacks. Odd smelly cheese, hunks of salami, and always one tradition disdained by my brother and I: the dreaded mushroom sandwiches. My parents are just fungi obsessed. These sandwiches are about as un-kid-friendly as you can imagine. Sautéed mushrooms, mixed with parsley, and slathered on buttered whole wheat bread. Combine this with a car with no air conditioning, a horribly boring side jaunt to the Shaker Museum, and you have an idea of our laborious trips to Maine as a child. Please try and picture the Shaker Museum. A whole set of Shaker wood chairs, lined up in a room. A Shaker white-hatted person escorts you, offering dry details about wood carving. A rousing chorus at the end sings "'Tis a gift to be simple" as you drive off (I exaggerate here). The point is, it was not fun.

My friend Nono came with us one year, she remembers the extreme discomfort of our backseat trifecta. We made the huge mistake of opening a jar of honey and spilling it across the seat, which wasn't such a fresh feel when sweltering in ninety degree weather. For a special lunch, we drove two hours out of our way to the Shartlesville Inn, which is still there. An all-you-can-eat Pennsylvania Dutch restaurant, where you sit family style with strangers at long picnic tables. Elephantine platters of food are brought upon you, mashed potatoes, stuffing, even something called filling, which is a combination of the two, as if we are mere sacks of cloth requiring an ingenious flocking to bring us to life. Pitchers of milk on each table to wash down the fried chicken and shoo-fly pie. Afterward, you waddle to the car, with its carcinogenic thermal air, thigh to thigh, observing patrons, I kid you not, barfing in the parking lot. We have one special incredibly bad feng-shui gas station we always seem to hit just as someone has an "attack" on the Jersey border. As I've said, a family of fragile stomachs and these attacks are frequent. The unfortunate placement of the stall is one foot away from the cash register, monitored by an extremely gruff Korean man. I think even part of the wall is missing, having been replaced by a small piece of thin particle board. We'd like something a bit comfier, but this horrible pit-stop is the only one available for many miles, and our stomachs uniformly lurch from the tainted diner food at about this time. Each year the Korean man seems angrier. Probably remembers us yearly as the loose-boweled family from down south. I don't even think we get gas there. We'll have to start bringing him a ham soon.

We often stop in Havre de Grace for a wonderful crab feast. And then there is *the tradition*: as soon as we get to Maine, we have to get a lobster roll. Now, I'm picky about these, we all are. Some like the plain lobster meat drizzled with butter. I do not. Some like a bit of celery. I do not.

Maine

I like a soft white roll, New England style (cut on the top, not the side). I like fresh, sweet lobster meat, of course, tossed lightly with mayo, salt, and pepper, and that's it. God forbid you put lettuce. Of course, once we actually hit the house, do we ever eat a lobster roll again? No, they're a bit of a teaser, a mere *amuse-gueule* in the ritual of the Maine trek. After that, we elevate ourselves to the whole crustacean and we never look back. Almost every night, we crack and suck these monsters, dripping with butter. Pure gluttony. Washed down with Pouilly-Fuissé or even beer, drenched in butter. Actually, I don't like lemon, it covers the flavor. I don't like lemon on any fish, as long as it is gleamingly fresh and pure. There is too much subtlety of flavor to mask with lemon, that's for fish that's old. And I love the green fat and the coral, as well, with their fumy ocean mineralness. There is a long running debate that never seems settled: soft shelled or hard. Now, I'm a soft sheller. With soft shells, of course, the shells are softer, catching them mid-molt and thus they tend to be a bit watery. So what? Let it drain. The point is, the meat is far sweeter. And the other plus is that most restaurants give you two soft shells. Others prefer the hard shell, stating the flesh is better. Any lobster, any time, is my motto, but only in Maine.

My grandparents sometime in the seventies bought a lovely old house in Bluehill, Maine, that had harbored two old schoolteacher spinsters most of their lives. The house came with every pan, every book intact, a lifetime complete. It had a nice old-fashioned kitchen, with yellowing cookbooks in a corner cupboard, a woodstove, a pantry, and a butler's pantry with rows of antique cut crystal, foggy from age. Out the back door of the kitchen was a separate guesthouse, rustically furnished, with tiny wooden single beds, scratchy blankets, another woodstove. It had the slight pine and mildew scent of all old vacation homes up north, a scent someone should manufacture and sell as "childhood nostalgia." Back behind the guesthouse was an old barn that housed my grandfather's Model T Ford car. What have I said about him? His name was Gene but we called him "Golly." First of all, he came from Long Island, Oyster Bay, the son of a famous judge in town—Judge O'Connor. He was remarkably handsome, up until the day he died at age eighty-six, as we all sat around him in a hospital in Charlottesville, Virginia, but that is a different story. As a teenager, I think he was a troublemaker, sweet-faced and reckless. He drank illegal gin, he chased girls, he terrorized all the servants of his grand house, he drove a brand-new Model T and would go into the city up to Harlem, to speakeasies, to dance to jazz. He dressed impeccably in the old way: Brooks Brothers, tweed, well tailored and immaculate. I remember him as a child dressing in a tuxedo, and wearing black patent leather slippers. They were odd and resembled the wide Mary Janes that Babar wore when he was decked out in his evening finery. In the Bahamas in winters, he turned gilded brown and wore Madras shorts, and pink oxfords. When he kissed you, he smelled pleasantly of Bay Rum. He was the picture of elegance. Most of his life he had worked for embassies and he and Nancy—and my mother and two uncles—lived in Thailand, Germany, Buenos Aires. I wasn't around in those years but the stories lingered. Their outrageous fights. They screamed and yelled their way around the world. And there was suspicion of affairs: I remember one day he came storming into the Middleburg house, Crednal: Nan, why don't you go up the stairs.

Later I learned from family gossip that Louis was a rich man they knew. My grandmother Nancy had once left my grandfather for him and flown in a jet with Louis, only to be miserable. She returned. Golly was no saint, he chased Thai servant girls, and there was even the question of men. It was a vague and insidious whisper, but there were signs: he returned to the U.S. and worked for the CIA for a while. One day he strangely was fired for something to do with conduct in a men's room. It was shadowy, secretive. Nancy was having panic attacks at the time, I don't know the truth. I shouldn't dredge out the family secrets, but we are all human beings, struggling, I know what I saw through my eyes, a larger-than-life man, ridiculously handsome in the classic, aquiline way as men in those days seemed to favor, a Fitzgerald-ish straight and long nose, hair slicked back and gleaming black, elegance, an assured and charming way at cocktail parties and gatherings, who would amuse us children by pulling out a fake bridge of teeth and becoming a werewolf.

And then there was the private, comfy side of him: a man who adored reading cookbooks like myself. Often, he was in the Maine kitchen when we'd stagger in, bleary-eyed in the morning, sitting in a faded chintz overstuffed chair, reading the old cookbooks, dressed in a proper robe, pajamas, and brown leather slippers.

Only on rare occasions would he venture to make something. He liked crab Louis (ironically), blueberry pie, and a lovely tomato-basil tart, which I think he got from Elizabeth David. I remember fondly one day we arrived weary from the horrible Maine car ride, fourteen hours from Virginia, with my small son, Ivan, who was tiny, born prematurely at six months, and Golly had made a crumbly blueberry pie, and a tiny mini tart for him.

. . .

I loved staying with them at this house. Across the way was the bay. We'd go out there and pick mussels from the rocks, and farther out, there were spiny sea urchins. We'd gather them in baskets, with gloves, and take them back to the house. They were a pain in the ass. We'd sprinkle them with soy sauce or smear them on buttered bread, French style. We'd steam the mussels and marinate them in a Spanish dressing. Through the years, my stepfather John has perfected this recipe—with chopped aromatics, herbs, and a Xerez sherry vinaigrette.

My brother joined the yacht club and sailed throughout the harbor or days were spent playing golf with the extremely ambitious players of my uncle and grandfather. After all, my grandfather grew up on the grounds of a golf course in Oyster Bay. But I did none of this. I was at home, doing the usual: reading or cooking. I don't think I've ever been far from these two activities. I would comb the extensive library of these two lady schoolteachers, and hang out in the shadowy house, while my grandmother, as usual, lay on her bed upstairs writing her novels on her manila pads. One was about an affair in Bangkok between an American woman and the king, a lush and sensual tale, and the other was about life in old-time Virginia. I never once thought I'd be a writer: this seemed too lofty and out of sight. I also spent hours drawing pictures of ladies and dresses, and I figured I'd be a painter. Most of them encouraged me to do this. I had an incredibly nineteenth-century upbringing, now that I think of it. I whiled away most of my life in a country estate, simply practicing my crafts—reading, writing poems, cooking, painting. I never went to the malls or attended gymnastic classes or piano or tennis as my friends did. I was solitary and quiet, as if I was reliving the country patrician lives of Jane Austen's characters. When my grandmother would emerge from her quarters, she might call me up. She'd let me have a piece of her jewelry that I coveted, she had stones from all over the world. Or, an item of clothing, and unlike my drab hippy mother, who wore no makeup and dressed in earth tones, my grandmother dressed in fuchsia and coral and Lilly Pulitzer. We shared the same sense of style and I adored it.

Then, we might venture into the small town of Bluehill. I would be hungry, looking back it seems that I was always hungry twenty-four hours a day and I still am. While others seem to forget about food, I am always thinking of it, ready for a nibble. My second son, Sunny, is exactly the same way. Sunny and I forage and drool all day long. We nibble, create, dream of food. In these jaunts to town, I would be longing for some fried clams or lobster roll, but my grandmother seemed to never, ever think of food. She was bejeweled, lipsticked, a deep tan. We'd buy gin or crabmeat from the local guy. I would be cooking dinner, an all-day event for me. She hated to cook, so it worked out fine. The boys would return. Ann and John from various jaunts to organic farms in the area or pottery places and I'd have made a feast—crab tart, mussels vinaigrette, a tomato salad with our own dragged up from Virginia.

If there's one thing a Virginian has to have besides ham, it's a fresh tomato from the garden. Pronounced "tomahto," by the way. I said I never saw Nancy eat—except two things. The first, when those summer tomatoes came, she'd make a sandwich—soft farm white bread, mayonnaise, salt and pepper, and slices of the still warm tomato caught between the slices. Sometimes I remember this eaten on the slightly sweet bread they make homemade in the Bahamas by two sisters who ran the Ruminette store, unsliced, you would carve a heavy slab of it and stud it with the tomato slices. She'd just sigh over this, and I get it. The second tomato joy was another Virginia favorite, fried green tomatoes. The ones in trendy restaurants are usually all wrong, often covered in a heavy, crunchy coating of cornmeal, which is disastrous. They should be dusted in plain old salt-and-peppered flour and fried in bacon fat. They caramelize around the crisp edges and ooze a sourness inside. We bring up a crate or two from Virginia just for this purpose as well.

It always comes back to my grandfather Eugene, in Maine. Thinking of the journey, I see him in the old worn chintz chair in the kitchen. Or sometimes, fresh from the golf course, golden and smiling. After he died in 2003, Nancy gave me a pile of papers he had scrawled, for me. It was a letter, dated from 2001. I had just published my first novel, which was a huge surprise for them. After all, Nancy was the writer. Gene had wanted to write as well. No one ever knew I would.

> *Dear Nani,*
>
> *To convey to what I think of your novel and you as a writer I resort to a jubilant expression from Down East Maine— Wicked Good! To deem* <u>Crawling at Night</u> *"wicked" is not the reaction of this man with a lifelong serious interest in a writer's craft. I leave "your wicked ways" to the millions of*

readers, sexual neophytes, and tsk tsk aficionados, who will doubtless make a great success for you and your publishers.

Rather, your novel returns me with great pleasure to thoughts of my early job with Charles Scribners and Sons where I was involved in publishing Fitzgerald and Hemingway. Hoping to be their successor, I examined with daily intentness every word, every paragraph of their skills in page proof.

Two wars and their aftermath in the Far East, South America, and Europe put me on a different path observing the great world in action, not in print.

I have ancient elitist publishing credentials for evaluating your skills as a writer— and I delight in them on every page.

You are assured as a writer. Your craft comes on full-fledged.

Is there a genetic component in your skills?

I am thinking of your grandmother Nancy's novels with their matchless richness and hypnotic subpoetry in conveying a fading regal Asian scene.

I have not finished your novel—what pleasures lay ahead!

Love, Golly

The rest of the papers are a series of recipes. Yes, we always, in the end, come back to food. Apparently, he thought we could write a cookbook together called "the Crawling at Night cookbook." A great idea, but one that ended with his death, since he never told me. But I have the recipes, and they are the style I knew Nancy and Gene for, the food of the islands, the thirties, eras gone by. People do not eat this way anymore, it has the flavor of the '21 Club and the drunken cook Carrie, from Bertha to the Oyster Bay Country Club. How do we as a family define a life? By what you ate, of course. Or better yet, by how you satisfied your hunger. And what was Gene's hunger? I do not know. I can only feebly guess with the tiny clues I picked up along the way. He loved to dance, they say, and he was the best. He hungered for fun, for life, for adventure. He loved beauty, and most of all, I believe he loved Nancy, despite all their shenanigans. He loved to eat and cook, he loved Bahamas fish chowder, crab Louis, jellied consommé, leg of lamb cooked until unrecognizably too done (he'd say: The French like it medium rare, I found out—we wanted to whisper, we do, too, but dutifully ate the gray flesh), blueberry tarts. He could mix a mean martini. He made coffee for his wife in his Brooks Brothers pajamas and brought it up to her.

In the end, it was his will, and specifically, the Maine house that tore our family asunder. I don't blame him. He left the beloved house to my uncle Harrison, and left my mother out—completely. She was understandably devastated and never spoke to Nancy again, or any of them for that matter. It's been years now. She had loved that house. We had thought we would be going forever. But it had disintegrated before then, their relationship. It was always rocky. My mother was not like them. She was different. They loved her, that I am certain. Not everyone is equipped to be parents, and I believe Harrison was someone more like them. He dressed like them and lived like them, and they enjoyed this. It is difficult to parent, more difficult when you are in separate worlds. Through the years after Owen was hospitalized, after Harrison married Moira, and Ann and John married and moved to Greenwood, imperceptible tensions arose. There were many causes: there was a lot of valuable land to handle and they simply turned this over to

Harrison. There weren't fights, there would be a relationship and then suddenly, nothing. Phone calls would be ignored by Ann, and Gene and Nancy would be out of our lives for a few years, and then they'd reconcile, and everyone would be back, instantly, without resolve or discussion. I don't know what the real root cause is in the rift, but I know there is pain and equally love on both sides. Sometimes, my grandmother calls me, begging me to talk to my mother. And I try, and then, it happens all over again. So now I've given up. But I have to notice, although I know they love her, why is their house full of photos of only Harrison, and not her or Owen?

In the end, they had reconciliated one more time, when Golly was dying. We all rallied. We were together as a big family again, in the hospital corridors, killing time, as he slowly was taken off medication and his breathing slowed. It took days, and we hung in clusters, in the halls, around the bed. Talking idly as if it were any cool spring and we had some time, as if years had not passed and we were at Crednal again. As if Moira, Harrison's wife, had not died of leukemia the year previous. As if Almond Tree House hadn't sold and we were sitting around on Cousin Fred's furniture, drinking rum before dinner. As if Owen was there, playing the Beatles, his shaggy hair in his eyes, laughing, before he was drugged up in the mental institution. We sat around the small single bed, where Gene lay. A last dosage of steroids had made his face a bit puffy, but he was still Golly and we watched him. He would take loud, swooshing breaths. The nurses said they didn't know how long it would take, a few days perhaps. It felt almost like a birth, the family sitting around, waiting. We joked a lot. Gaga was with us, Harrison's boys, then men in their twenties, Burr, Dana, and Levin. We discussed their lives, Burr working in China. Teased him about getting married. Dana, a lawyer in Los Angeles, Levin an actor in L.A. as well. It became so comfortable after a while, as if it really was back in the old days. It was the matter of forced no-air time between us, no real agenda except the very big one of looming death, but we are a repressed lot, and we pretty much avoided any emotional reminder of that. I think because of Moira's tragic death this whole process was too fresh for Harrison and the boys, no doubt incredibly painful, so they played stoic and laughed in their soft, easy laughter. Harrison viewed it all clinically, as if a machine was breaking down. At one point the group had gone to get sandwiches, he and I remained. He told me, in his easy, soft Virginia accent, at this point, he's pretty much checked out. He's functioning, breathing, but Golly isn't here. He's a set of reflexes right now. I could go pull the cord out and he—ahhhhunrh, my grandfather let out a huge, argumentative cough at this exact point—and we laughed. So much for being "checked out."

I think he was floating in and out, in that dreamy twilight we experience as if we are inadvertently falling asleep at a dinner party. You want to be part of the action, but you are so tired, you catch snippets and pieces of conversation and meld it with your dream world. Sometimes someone might snap you out of it by addressing you directly, but you are pretty much falling away. My ex-husband perfected this—we called it "martining." The reason I call it that is because in the middle of a family dinner party he was nodding off and suddenly woke to a start and said, "Purple martins!" Of course, we were discussing the role of shallots in a proper beurre blanc or some such, nothing to do with the impetuous local birds, setting us into a riot of snortles, and thus coining the term forever.

We ate sandwiches in the hospital room, watched Robert De Niro on *Inside the Actors Studio* until my grandmother brought us back to reality. This wasn't the Almond Tree House living room, this was death, and we would assume the somber silence and respect again. There is a tendency for life to always just burst forward, giddily, but in this situation you are supposed to pretend that life is quiet and shy, or that death is, more likely.

He dragged on, gasping, pausing for a minute, gasping again. It seemed uncomfortable. The nurse finally told us, you have to tell him it's okay to go. Kind of a cliché but these nurses have seen a lot of death. People hold on, she said. The problem was obvious to us all, silently—would we take care of Gaga, as he had done so well? There was much animosity in the family, back and forth. An inability to simply care and love for each other, as if that would be an ugly Hallmark card. A distaste for sentimentality, but really, a terror. Therefore, would she also be outcast and thrown away if he left, like Owen, Ann, the others?

But we held him on all sides, and told him this. We would take care of Gaga. His breathing became slower and slower, and finally, stopped. He stopped breathing. A minute went by. The heart still palpitated under his chest. Then, all movement ceased, and just like the ephemeral waste of a sunset ebbing in fleeting streaks, the color of his skin shifted from red to pink to purple to green, blue, gray, and then, within minutes solidified to granite. At this point, we summoned my grandmother, who couldn't be there for that, and she came in shocked. Who is this man? she said. He looks like a farmer.

Now, Ann and John, my brother and I go to a new town in Maine called Bayside in our cluster and Harrison goes to Nancy and Gene's old house in Bluehill in his cluster. Owen goes nowhere.

We deal with these changes, as we do with all changes, by eating and laughing and being ephemeral as we are, because that's all we have. I am leaving for Maine in a month. I've started researching the lobster roll stop.

Writing the packing list, with basmati rice, saffron, barbari bread, dried lemons, and rosewater included, because I'm going with Persians, and life always changes, and the palate changes as well. There were years where I brought black beans and smoked meats, farofa and cachaça, because I was immersed in Brazil. Or, sometimes I'll drag along a throng of curry spices, my little burned chapati pan, and mustard oil. For countless years, I traveled with a sushi mat, sushi vinegar, and a prized sashimi knife. I have traveled through countries by the route of the stomach, sometimes literally, like trips to Maine and sometimes, merely through a vague approximation, a mini journey, into someone's kitchen.

❖ **Lobster Rolls**

> Meat of 2 lobsters, cut into chunks
> Hellman's mayonnaise

Salt and pepper
Soft New England–style (split top) hot dog buns, warmed

Toss lobster meat with the mayonnaise and season to taste. Pile into warm buns and enjoy.

❖ Fried Green Tomatoes

Flour
Salt and black pepper
Fresh green tomatoes, cut into ¼-inch slices
Vegetable oil for frying

Mix flour and a little salt and pepper to taste in bowl. Coat each tomato slice with flour. Let sit for 30 minutes.

Heat oil in a skillet to medium-high. Add tomatoes. Adjusting heat when necessary, let tomatoes brown on one side, then turn and brown on the other. When tomatoes are a golden brown, remove one at a time and place on paper towels to drain.

❖ Mushroom Sandwiches

1 pound white button mushrooms, thinly sliced
Olive oil
Salt and pepper
Juice of a lemon
2 tablespoons chopped parsley
Soft whole wheat bread
Butter

Sauté mushrooms in olive oil. Add salt and pepper to taste, lemon juice, and parsley. Let cool. Spread two pieces of bread with butter, add a few tablespoons of filling—enjoy.

❖ Golly's Blueberry Pie

Blueberry Filling
⅔ cup granulated sugar
1 tablespoon brown sugar
3 tablespoons all-purpose flour
1 tablespoon Minute Tapioca
⅛ teaspoon ground nutmeg
1 teaspoon lemon juice
1 tablespoon butter or margarine, cut into bits
4 cups Maine wild blueberries (fresh)

Crusts
2 cups all-purpose flour, plus some for dusting
¼ cup cake flour
1 teaspoon salt
¼ teaspoon baking powder
⅓ cup plus 1 tablespoon shortening
5 tablespoons ice water
Sugar for dusting
Lemon juice for sprinkling

To make berry filling, combine sugars, flour, tapioca, nutmeg, lemon juice, and butter in a bowl. Toss with berries. Set aside.

To make crusts, sift flours into bowl with salt and baking powder. Cut in shortening to make a fine meal to ensure tenderness and flakiness. Add ice water, a tablespoon at a time. Toss with fork until dough starts to form a ball. Form into a ball and divide in half. Roll out one half of the dough for the bottom crust. Dust with sugar and flour. Fill crust with berry mixture. Sprinkle with lemon juice and dot with butter. Roll out top crust and place over filling. Flute edges and cut slits in top crust. Decorate with berries and leaves cut from leftover dough.

Bake at 400°F for 40 to 50 minutes, till golden.

Chapter 6

The Iranian Kitchen

Saffron and Rosewater, 2005

You could say I've traveled to Iran, at least through the stomach. This foray actually starts at the front door, where you are greeted by a small weaving of Allahu Akbar on the wall and the sweet, high-pitched mingle of nutty rice and saffron. You should take your shoes off as well and tread the hall in white socks. You should be carrying roses, if you know what's good for you. I have come because I am the date of an Iranian man, who wishes to introduce me to his friends and culture. As the years go by, I become a friend, well known and trusted. An American who understands their culture. Through these times, I have felt as if I have been a student of the culture, the food, the manners. And yet, the perspective is always a subtly of an older culture merging and mingling in the midst of a boorish younger culture, the U.S.

Entering the living room, you will be greeted by warm handshakes. If you are a man, kiss women if you wish. depending on how European you view yourself, you can kiss men on both cheeks or just chastely shake their hands. You are walking on intricate rugs from Isfahan, or Shiraz. They cover every corner of the house. Everyone will be well dressed, gleaming, powdered, made-up, bejeweled. Sitting politely, awaiting your arrival. You will feel as if the Queen of England will soon arrive, but this is merely a dinner party, a mingling of all ages, children politely emerging from deep in the basement to have their cheeks pinched, their small hands shaken, their heads kissed and stroked. The child is adored in Persian culture in a visceral way, touched, handled, kissed, in a way we fear.

If you are like me, an American, a blond American, you are a stranger and you are studied. You are assumed perhaps to have libertine manners, and be ignorant of their culture. It isn't unusual. Most Americans are unaware of the difference between Persians and Arabs, and especially to the difference in all the culture. I can only offer my small, no doubt biased observations and they all relate to either food or love, my favorite subjects.

My favorite foods in the world are caviar, quormeh sabzi, Persian greens stew, and saffron and rosewater ice cream. All three come from the Caspian Sea region. The stew is so bracing and sharp, full of sour dried lime, and a mixture of fresh chopped herbs cooked for hours with lamb. It is heaven, it is sheer pleasure, and it mingles in my mouth with love, for a man from Persia taught it to me, and I watched him, his dark eyes hooded, as he sautéed lamb for me, chopped herbs for me, and you know how sensitive I am to food, and to being cooked for, and to Persian food, so I was a goner from the start.

When you are seated, there are the polite and tempered

questions, such as would you like some tea? You are offered a clear glass of boiling hot amber liquid, fragrant with smoky bergamot or orange flowers. Small sweets, shirini, that reek of orange water, roses, and almonds are passed around. Lemon-soaked pistachios are proffered. Tiny kernels of orange blossoms coated in sugar, and these ones are accompanied by jokes, since they are the candy of weddings. Paper-thin crystallized sugar wafers, pulaki, embedded with dried lime. A bar candy, called sofran, slightly crumbly with a caramel and saffron flavor. Hunks of broken gaz, a white nougat-like candy made from bark. It goes on and on. How come nobody knows about this stuff? I'm into food and Persian food is widely unknown, but so intense and redolent of perfumes and lingering on the senses. And these are only the appetizers. It is the Persian custom to first serve tea and sweets to the guests, since alcohol is forbidden in Islam. But then, they break into that about five seconds later, when they offer you wine or liquor and some savory appetizers break through—pickles, olives, the very delicious and universal salad-e olivieh, your basic doctored-up potato salad with chicken, carrots, peas, and sour pickles, lime juice. Tiny sour pickles, olives, stuffed grape leaves (the Persian version is oddly sweet). After all of this, in an hour or so, the platters of food arrive, and in order of importance, there is rice.

First of all, let me make it clear, I am not a rice eater per se. It's not my favorite starch, I'll take a hot starchy potato tasting of earth, with a good crackle of sea salt anytime. And I do adore my sushi, and the rice is the most important component of that, so I can go there. But in terms of beans and rice, no. Indian rice, not bad to mop up a nice Goan curry. Chinese rice? The least appealing. But I have a soft spot for Persian rice. And insane new comfort food has expanded on my horizon, chelo kabob, which is the equivalent to burger and fries to Americans or fish and chips to the English. Fluffy, delicate basmati rice, with a trickle of saffron and a bit of butter, served with a grilled roll of kubideh (flavored ground meat) and a few quarters of grilled tomato. Sprinkle this as the Persians do with the sourish sumac powder (which reduces cholesterol) and dig in. But this is just the beginning of Persian rice. Back to our dinner, they will serve several different platters. One will be plain, to be served with the various khoresht (stews) they might serve. Another, served with braised lamb shanks in saffron, will be the adored baghali polo, a dill and fava bean pilaf. Or perhaps the colorful zeresht polo, a neon tone of saffron studded with tiny bright crimson barberries, tart baby versions of cranberries, served usually with a chicken of some sort.

Rice is not easy to make, we all have our bad experience of the gloppiness that can result. It takes a bit of practice. Thus the creation of rice cookers. And Persian rice is no exception. It's taken me a good three years to really get it down. First, you must wash basmati rice five times, until "clean," which means the water runs clear and not cloudy. It would then behoove you to soak it for a couple of hours first with a lot of salt, two table-spoons. Then, you rinse this, add new water, and boil and watch this with direct attention. Don't answer the phone, don't go take a shower: watch. As it starts to float to the surface in about seven minutes, taste a kernel. If it is slightly soft with just a tiny bit of al dente in the center, remove and drain. Pour oil in your pan in order to create the delectable Persian tah-dig, or rice crust, which they all seem to adore, and I've known Persians who have actually broken teeth from this habit. Put the rice back in a pyramid shape, drizzle a spoonful or two of water on top, cover in two paper towels, a firm lid, and let it cook at medium for a while. When you hear a slight sizzle, pull the heat down to low. Let it sit for twenty to thirty minutes. Enjoy beautiful rice.

The fact that I know how to make this, or quormeh sabzi as well as if not better than most Persians, confuses them, because they had me pegged. Who is she? There seems to be little confusion in the world of women, little ambiguity; marriageable or not. Marriage is the key of all Persian society. It is discussed, joked about, whispered about, avoided, but it is the essence of all female-male transaction. A date is a decision, instant, a yes or no. And marriage is usually preferred with an Iranian, but the odd farangi slides in. The ones who are innocent or foolish, or just plain adventurous. The traditional marriage is like buying a Mercedes-Benz. It is a bargain. The man offers wealth, position, family, then hopefully attractiveness. The woman offers beauty, education, virginity, family. Though the virginity factor is fading, and still, how can you define virginity? The current trend is a physical foray into anything but penetration, things we may blush about, as long as the hymen is intact. Is this true virginity?

So, here I am, a writer with some acclaim, very American, independent, divorced, two children, defiant, yet, I can make Persian food and host as well as any Persian khanom (lady). I speak a smattering of Farsi and I know ta'rouf (manners). I confuse.

My Persian friends will ask me, over bits of the saffrony food, over sips of the ubiquitous Pepsi (where is the Gewürtztraminer that would so balance this food?) do I think they are terrorists? Did I like that horrible movie *Not Without My Daughter*? Did I enjoy *Farenheit 9/11*? What kind of books do you write? In

Iran, most of our books are forbidden. I am not sure what to say, my books are sensual forays into the hearts of men, usually through sex or food. I write fiction, I say. They are cautious and mistrustful of us, and yet, they love Americans and this country. They've learned to weave their cultural threads around Costco and Neiman Marcus, their two favorite stores. They will complain about our government and our lack of relaxation, and yet, who can relax in the traffic that is slowly suffocating Tehran? Iran, like anybody who lives away from their original country, has become a place of old dreams—how in the springtime new year the people walk the streets in their finery, the bonfires, the beauty of the women, the taste of the ambrosial fruit, the solidity of the houses built from stone not plastic, the innocence of the people who do not snatch children to kill.

Oh, we all live in dream castles, especially me: I sit in the house, polite, enjoying the lovely saffron ice cream now, washed down with more amber tea, and a woman sings a lovely ragged sura in her earthy voice, I know no words but laugh politely when everyone seems to laugh. I can see flecks of who we used to be in Persians, they are a different species, a people honed from thousands of years of culture, flung into this giant plastic mall called America, with glossy women as appealing and dangerous as candy. But we all try, with kisses and warmth and smiles. We are human, at least. And food seems to be a way people can quietly and surreptitiously love each other, without too much of a fuss. The person who carefully chopped the mountains of herbs, strained the saffron, boiled the tea, removed the sticky skin from the blue-skinned lamb shanks did so with the sole purpose of bringing joy and kindness all around them. There

was not competition or spite, reclamation or bragging. A lovely herb-flecked baquali polo, fragrant and soft, filling everyone's mouths, needs no translation. A taste of fava bean—the ancient bean of the Middle East, brought from Egypt—the dillweed a horn of spring, the luxury of saffron and butter. It is a silent caress for every guest that says, You are here with me and this is what I offer, this is good and for you, I wish to care for you.

The last of the tea is drunk, all the fruit carved and bitten and enjoyed, the last song sung, the Iranian kitchen now houses the older husband dutifully scrubbing the rice pans and the large platters. Younger people leave in their small cars with cheshmeh had (evil eye) hanging from the mirror, and the two older ladies who never married softly kiss my face. There are long goodbyes in the Iranian kitchen. The night is dark, and crickets are loud by the holly bushes out front. In the evening in the suburban neighborhood, a Korean couple waves from their car next door. A few stars are visible in the sky. I will drive exhausted, yet with the same fullness one feels at the airport when returning from a trip to a faraway land—many tastes, many new ideas, packed in containers to gently open and revisit in solitude. To see how they feel upon yourself, to warp them, re-create them.

After the proud host has cleared the crystal glasses with his wife and they scrape the rice pan in the kitchen and after the candles have been snuffed, rice kernels fastidiously picked up from the Isfahan rug, he will know his heart and head, his knowledge of people is different from mine.

He has lived differently and from this gathered many ideas in a bundle he refers to as his heart. Sometimes, perhaps, driving back from his job at IBM, he remembers his neighbor and the best friend of his mother during his youth. Often, he would go to her house covered by rosebushes and knock on the door. She was always glad to see him. He would take off his shoes, pad in the carpeted house, and sit quietly at that familiar table covered in a large plastic sheet over a lace tablecloth. Fruit would be put out for him and a cold glass of Pepsi. As he grew older and became a young man, a hot glass of amber tea. Jaleh-khanom, her ankles so swollen, almost gelatinous, would shuffle to the kitchen in socks and slippers, scuffed manicured hands, her hair in a silk scarf and ladle out something to the boy, but in this particular fantasy she has a large platter of bright yellow rice studded with tart barberries and pistachios and soft roasted chicken that falls off the bone, and yogurt with shallots, a chopped salad, and a pile of raw herbs for nibbling, and her son, who is an unmarried engineer and lives with her, comes in and joins them, and they laugh, about movies, jokes, girls, marriage, politics.

I come to their house with my own bundle, long hot days in Virginia, ham in soft rolls, sweet iced tea, the sound of The Beatles over and over. And yet, we shake hands, we kiss, we smile.

As I left, they placed in my hand, one real container, on the car seat: a small Tupperware rectangle, filled with a portion of baqali polo, lamb, another with a scoop of salad-e olivieh. So tomorrow, for lunch, I will once again linger in the land of saffron and roses.

❖ Qormeh Sabzi

Traditionally this is made with fresh herbs, though most Iranians nowadays use a dried herb mix available in Persian shops. I use a combination of the two—the fresh herbs lighten and sweeten the dish, the dried herbs and intensity as well as the needed fenugreek, which is hard to find fresh. I use frozen spinach because fresh tends to become slimy in this dish. Serve hot with basmati rice.

2 large onions, diced
1½ pounds lamb, cut into 2-inch pieces
5 tablespoons vegetable oil, or more as needed
½ teaspoon turmeric
Salt
¼ teaspoon black pepper
8 whole dried Persian limes (*limu-omani*)
2 cups finely chopped fresh parsley
2 bunches scallions
1 cup finely chopped fresh cilantro
2 cups dried *qormeh sabzi* herbs (with fenugreek)
1 cup chopped frozen spinach, thawed and squeezed dry
½ teaspoon saffron, crushed and dissolved in 1 tablespoon
    hot water
1 cup cooked kidney beans
1 tablespoon butter

In a pot, brown onions with meat in 3 tablespoons of the oil. Be sure and let the meat and onions become a nice caramel brown. This will take some time, but will add a rich flavor. Add 2 cups water, turmeric, salt, and pepper. Using a fork, puncture four of the dried lemons and add to the pot. Crush with the palm of your hand the other four and also add. Bring to a simmer.

In a skillet, fry the parsley, scallions or chives, and cilantro in 2 tablespoons of the oil over medium heat for 20 minutes, stirring constantly, until they are darkened and crispy. Add *qormeh sabzi* herbs. Add the spinach and cook until browned. Add to the meat mixture along with the saffron and let gently simmer for 2 hours.

Add kidney beans and simmer for another half hour. I like to round out the flavors by checking for salt and pepper at the end and adding a tablespoon of butter, mixing well until blended.

❦ Bademjoon Khoresht

6 small black eggplants, each about 4 inches long
Salt
¾ cup olive oil
1 white onion, diced
1½-pound leg of lamb, cut into 2-inch cubes
2 cups water
Tomato paste
1 cup chunky crushed tomatoes, preferably organic
½ teaspoon turmeric
Black pepper
3 medium tomatoes, sliced
1 cup pickled unripened grapes, available in Persian shops
    (substitute 3 tablespoons lime juice)

Peel the eggplants, leaving a small trace of skin here and there and also leaving the stems. Cut each eggplant in half lengthwise and sprinkle with salt and set aside. Leave for an hour. Meanwhile, in a heavy 12-inch skillet, heat ½ cup of the olive oil over moderate heat until a light haze forms above it. Add the onion and the lamb cubes to the pan and sauté until a rich caramel brown. Add the unripened grapes and sauté. Add the water, tomato paste, crushed tomatoes, turmeric, 1 teaspoon salt, and a few grindings of pepper. Bring to a boil over high heat, meanwhile scraping into the pan the brown particles clinging to the bottom and sides of the pan. Reduce the heat to low, and simmer tightly covered for 45 minutes.

Arrange the eggplant halves side by side on top of the lamb and place the tomato slices over them. Cover tightly again and simmer for about 45 minutes longer, until the eggplant and lamb are tender. Taste for seasoning and serve at once from a deep heated platter or bowl. Serve with rice.

Chapter 7

Peru

Muy Criollo/Gossamer Meringue, 2003

I was astonished, at age ten, by my grandfather Francis in his late seventies traveling to Machu Picchu by himself. I remember him sitting on the lawn, wearing an ascot, knickers, and smoking a tiny cigar, while he told us the story of this ancient ruin. I, though, was curious about who he went with and what he ate. You'll notice, in this book, an obsession with these two topics, both of which were unsatisfied on this day. Was it the mysterious lover he kept in Washington? He blew a small column of incensed smoke toward us, as we sat on the lawn overlooking the shaggy horses. "Great swarms of wild parrots flew over us," he said.

Thirty years later, here I am in Peru, looking for the wild parrots and more.

We descended into Lima in a cloud. In fact, Lima remained so the entire time we were there, inchoate, wispy, the opposite of the pea-soup analogy, more like drifting through gossamer meringue. Immediately, we ate, then slipped around the shiny cobblestone side roads around the Palacio de Justicio, made of black river rock and resembling black beans. En route there was a man selling tiny steaming quail eggs, a woman and her mother hawking beef heart skewers, and a chicken rotisserie shop, ubiquitous throughout Peru, golden hues of crackling roasted chicken, such comfort food after a cold, antiseptic flight across the Atlantic, and those plastic mini tubs of microwaved brown gravy, plastic wrapped rolls. Chicken, crispy, cooked over coals, with homemade chunky fried potatoes and a sharp green chile sauce and lots of syrupy sangria. Slight drunkenness, laughter, grease. The whole place rumbled with harsh Lima Spanish and cumbia music throbbed hard and tinny as noisy car engines sang from the streets.

He told me he would not make love to me this night, but tomorrow, watch out. He said it several times, watch out tomorrow, he said, like a seventeen-year-old boy, I'm drunk, Nani, I'm drunk! I would like to tell you who you are to me, but I am not even sure how to phrase it, because we have been lovers, friends, and remain in between, drifting together when we are single, apart when we find others, attached yet unattached. He is someone very dear to me, and yet impossible to embrace fully.

His voice became louder and more metallic. I said cool down. People are looking.

I'm not going to make love to you tonight.

Okay, okay, you've made that clear.

But tomorrow, watch out.

Okay.

I wonder what they marinate these chicken in. Can I ask the recipe?

I tried to figure out drunkenly how to say it. Receita? Because I lived in Brazil the two languages always mixed.

I'm drunk!

Eat more of those fries.

Walking back, wobbling, we inadvertently entered a sad gay bar by the corner, thinking it to be a salsa club. Sad because it was merely a room, without color or lights, and it played throbbing, electrified techno music that seemed mechanical and he went to use the bathroom, and I met four very young boys who gave me champagne and asked my age and then he came back and said let's go, I hate this place.

A year later, I dreamt of that small club, that there was a special room in the front for the older men, who sat in chairs like old retirees and watched the young ones through a special window. I asked him, was there a room like that just last week? What are you talking about, he said? I wonder why I dreamt about that room. Are we too old now, shut away from youth?

When we came back to the Sheraton, there was a sea of Limeños, dark and glossy throughout the hotel, their very shininess impressed me, like small mink, and a spectacular woman sung in a red satin sheath in a casino, I didn't catch the lyrics, I just heard amor, amor, amor.

He unfolded his clothes and stood in his white underwear, his tiny, compact body, older than mine, foreign, scary. I came up behind him and held his small waist, delicate and small like someone eighteen years old and he cautioned me, not tonight.

• • •

In the morning, we ate alpaca ham and passion fruit in the Sheraton lounge and watched the World Cup with a few impassioned Brazilians. The alpaca was lean, like venison, smoky and very salty. We both ate copious amounts of it, watched Brazil get killed by France, and then walked the cloudy city to the cathedral. He held my hand without passion, as if a part of him lay dormant and unearthed. I held him tight at times, or kissed his forehead, which was cooler than the rest of him and salty. Tonight I'm going to kill you, he said.

We were hungry and I begged for ceviche, the national dish of Peru. A distinguished-looking gentleman in tweed had recommended El Mordisco, which they found to be a bustling barlike atmosphere in Miraflores. Order for me, he insisted, and I ordered the Russian salad, a favorite I compared in all the countries, in Brazil potatoes mashed with tuna, egg, and carrots in mayonnaise, in Iran, salad-e olivieh, potato with mayonnaise, lime, pickles, eggs, and chicken, and here, fresh chunks of potato, beet, carrot, tossed in a light mayonnaise, with whole eggs. Then, came the pearl, a luscious, overflowing platter of fruits of the sea, red snapper chunks, octopus, sea urchin, spiny lobster, baby clams, mussels, scallops with their bright scarlet roe. All drenched in lime and red onion and spicy aji chile pepper, with a chunk of corn and some cold steamed sweet potato. We devoured it, exclaimed, sighed. Finished it with cold beer, dried slated corn. Then, full and lethargic, we walked through the neighborhood and came upon the seaside, wild, foamy and gray, below mossy cliffs. Couples hung by the edge of the walls over the ocean and clawed each other desperately, grabbing. We are not at the first stage of passion nor are we in the settled comfort of the married couple. We are in romantic limbo, and always shall be. Underneath the walkway, we found a mall bustling with activity. Teenagers and rich Limeños strolled around amid Tony Roma's Ribs and Starbucks and gelato shops. Above them, a glassy Marriott loomed over the ocean.

He had started again. You're history tonight. Watch out.

We drank cappuccinos and ate terrible cheesecake, limp and wobbly with gelatin.

We walked more and more. We stopped sometimes by the water and talked about my boyfriends, his girlfriends, my children, his work, his friends, her friends, and sometimes, that he loved her, and then they talked about the definition of that word, how he loved her but not like when he was younger, with his Danish girlfriend, because he missed her all the time, and he didn't miss her all the time. So maybe you don't love me, I said. That's it, you don't love me. It's okay, I'm a big girl. I can handle it. He said nothing. The ocean was louder now and they could feel the air and tiny pieces of water that came in small gushes and felt delicate, inexplicable, like fairy breath. But in that moment I loved him intensely because of history and the ocean. Because he stood here with me and saw the Pacific. Or because he is the only one I know in an entire country. I wish it was that simple, but this is and isn't. The why is so hard to define, and for that reason, for me, this is real love, a vague and ever present mist.

Hours had passed since the ceviche. We were hungry again.

We could either eat or make love. We would eat.

A taxi driver told us of a great restaurant by the water. I will take you there, he said. In the car, we held hands. I looked at his tight, small thighs, everything about him was small and perfect. He is exactly my height. I kissed him, his neck, his face. I was hungry for him, so I ate ceviche, and more ceviche and ice cream and alpaca and roasted chicken, and I wanted him, to taste him, to eat him, to bite him, to swallow him. I wanted him to shave his chest, which was so thick it felt like the tough fibrous filters I put in our air-conditioning unit, I wanted him to shave so I could lick his salty body and taste all of him, but instead, we ate Lima.

The taxi driver brought us to a large, brightly lit restaurant over the sea, and I ran in and spoke to the owner and checked it out. It was large, cavernous, and the only people there were giant mob of senior Americans brought in by a bus. The air had the familiar warm sour tang of a school cafeteria. We have to get out of here, I said to him. It's touristy.

He didn't even look in.

Mi esposa esta muy picky, he said to the driver. They laughed.

I want a place that's really Peruvian, I said. Muy criollo.

Criollo? he nodded, turned the car around, yo se.

But the place was closed. He tried another place, another obvious tourist trap so they got out in the mist and we walked and walked.

I want ceviche again, I said.

I want you, he said, and kissed me slowly.

He lived in a brick rambler and ate cookies with tea. He smelled of cinnamon when he kissed her. He spent hours in the bathroom, and his feet were smaller than hers. This is a man I dated just after my divorce. We met the first night I ever tried a salsa class. We had to switch partners, and he popped up from nowhere, his hands in front of him like a seal. I remember he was charming, funny, but too small for me. Too finicky and anal. I felt friendly toward him and when he suggested we go out dancing sometime, I said, yes. I went in casually and got stuck. I have tried to move on and I always go back to him, eventually.

A new taxi driver told us he knew a better spot, the best place for ceviche. It was sleek and modern, cement and bamboo, a river ran through the restaurant.

We ordered two different ceviches, pisco sours, and a large mashed potato ball stuffed with seafood, and an inky paella in a cast iron pot. The ceviche here was more delicate, more Japanese. In fact, the restaurant was fashioned to be part sushi bar, part cevicheria, a blend of the culture of Lima's tradition and the sleek, new modernity of the Japanese aesthetics, since Peru boasts a heavy Japanese population. We ordered one type of just shellfish, lightly washed in lime, and another with barely cooked chunks of corvino in a cilantro sauce.

As he chewed on shrimp shells and rubbed my shoulder, the entire restaurant started clapping. We looked around, astonished. What's going on? I asked a waiter, noticing a group of men who had everyone's attention.

Is it a futbol player? Coach? I asked, because Peru was enthralled in the World Cup.

No, señora, said the waiter. Es El Presidente.

The president of Peru?

Si, señora.

We were shocked, and watched families, children, women, all surround him, kissing, sitting on his lap, getting autographs, shaking hands, flashes going off in every direction. I pulled out my camera and approached the group and begged a photo in bad Spanish.

Yes, of course, said El Presidente. He was a small man, yet solid, and his face was dark red, heavy set, as if he had been parboiled.

We squeezed together, and some children got into the picture, and they smiled, and through his teeth, he whispered, tonight, you're dead. You're history.

As it turned out, he had diarrhea and I watched bad Reggaetón videos and we went to bed early because in the morning we had to catch a flight to Cusco. It was strange leaving the city of clouds. As usual, flying made me nervous and I wanted to take a beta blocker but they were packed in my suitcase, but he oddly made me feel safe, something about the way he always logically saw the world separate from his heart irritated me, but on a plane I needed that cool, analytical view. I clung to his hand. I leaned against him. First, we were in clouds and then just blue air and all of a sudden, we descended into a different world, brown and white mountain peaks of startling clarity and devoid of all civilization. Mile after mile of Andes, spectacular and lonely at the same time. I fantasized occasionally about falling into these mountains, crashing, but his presence brought me back to the safe world of his science. I fantasized about altitude sickness, and how I might get one of the crushing diseases of the lungs or brain ("unusually painful headache") and quickly realized I could let myself descend into a panic, so I floated back to his safeness and wondered when he would make love to me, and watched the Andes and then we were in Cusco, careening through a town jackhammered and kinetic with festival, colors and flags and dancing—Inti Haymi, festival of the sun—celebrated on the summer solstice. He then buried his head in my hair as we walked through the parade and said, I love you.

If Peru has a smell, which it certainly does, all my luggage bled this scent when I returned, it is the warm husky wood of a strange incense they burn and the slightly funky foot smell of the coca tea they press into your hand everywhere, including the airport of Cusco, where they greet in Andean garb (the odd fedora, the bright embroidered dirndl skirt, and the somber Incan face, proud, long, angular, bright red cheeks against the brown skin).

In the Andes, the food is all about corn, potatoes in all types, especially the dark, turdlike purple varieties, aji chile peppers, quinoa, and notably, the guinea pig, which is raised in Peruvian backyards like chickens. By eight that evening, we sat in a restaurant in front of a blazing fire drinking pisco sours and the waiter cheerfully brought us a whole guinea pig, deep-fried, mounted on oranges, stuffed with wild Andean aromatics, and decorated with a toothpick skewered with maraschino cherries and oranges on his head.

The taste, however, was oily and stale, unfortunately or maybe fortunately, since satisfying an urge for this delicacy would be difficult in the States. Scouring Petco for dinner material is not a happy idea. He suggested it tasted like Kentucky Fried Chicken skin, I suggested deep-fried felt. Neither of us was impressed. We drowned our taste buds in coca tea, and the ubiquitous chocolate cake, and I thought of sex, how, where, most important, when.

Here I am three years later, after the salsa. We dated for a while, six months or so. I didn't care if he was short, or if he wore a wig that he took off every night and rested on a white Styrofoam head and then pasted to his skull every day. I didn't care if he spent hours in the bathroom every day. It was his eyes. They looked tired and Persian, like ancient Sassanian paintings, an almost Asian curve to the edge. And his small dark hands, perfect and soft, with tendons popping out on the tops. He was so lovely naked, like a young Arab boy. The smell of his body is like Turkish incense and grass.

I don't want to marry you, he had said. Okay, I said, broken-hearted, but not sure why marriage was the issue so soon. Three weeks later, I went dancing with a young Egyptian friend, and saw him there. After, the Egyptian and I went to a hookah bar and had lamb curry at two in the morning. He drove to my house and got in the door. When I came home I said goodbye to the Egyptian, and came in to my house. When I walked upstairs there was an apple on my bed. Someone was knocking on the door downstairs and my dog was frantic. It was him, with tears in his eyes. He'd been spying from the bushes. He came back, for then. It always came down to the same thing: I can't marry you. Eventually, we broke up and dated other people. We kept in contact through holidays and birthdays.

One day I went for tea in his small rambler that smells like Persian herbs, lined with Tabriz rugs and old lady chotchkes. I can't see me living there. He has bad art, Thomas Kinkade, artist of Light crap. Small cottages aglow in the countryside. He buys shampoos and lotion in bulk from Costco. He is completely practical, while I am completely romantic. He is insanely organized, I am scattered. Left brain, right brain. But, in bed, he is the softest, gentlest man in the world.

. . .

We go the train station to go to Machu Picchu but the trains are
on strike. Apparently, some coca workers have lain on the
tracks in protest. We talk to some young hikers from England
who plan on walking on the tracks. We give it a thought, but
decide that, at forty, we're too old for this stuff. He gets really
depressed and keeps saying, I can't believe I can't see Machu
Picchu. I keep saying let's find something else to do, so we go to
other ruins, and spend the day cruising around Cusco markets
and then, tired and dusty, reeking of burned coca leaves, we go
to our room, and we bought candles in the market, small im-
ages of the Almighty Virgin, and incense that smells like dark
cedar from Lebanon, and the hotel room is a painted a dark
sixties orange and you can hear cumbia music from faraway,
and the curtains are yellowed and muslin and they sway slightly
in the stale air conditioning and and his mouth tastes cold and
watery, like a stream in the Andes. My shirt is taken off slowly,
as you would for a weary child, and I can't get past the thicket
on his chest and he is always salty on his forehead, and he is an
ocean, a river, and as you go lower, a jungle, and all the warmth
of his smell is who he is. Our bodies are exactly the same length,
but I am bigger and softer and I wrap him up. We are floating
on some place where your tongues meet and your lips brush,
but your mind is far away, you are both here and in another
place, and the smell of other lands is coming through the windows, and ancient voices are in the air, and it all comes back
quickly to where we are when I see his blackened eyes in front
of me, and that particular smile he only seems to smile at the
exact moment after he has entered me and looks for the first

time at me, open and saying, here it is. And then he begins what I can only feel is primal and old as water, this rhythm, this pounding, this intensest unrest, going into me deeper and deeper, until we get to the point where he screams loud, louder than if I took a sword through his heart. And then such, killed, he sprawls to the side. And the incense of Pachamama fills the air.

And then, the young men, with the long, dark faces, brown and worried, with the river-carved hands, rise from the tracks, rubbing the burrows in their flesh caused by the metal blades of the tracks. They speak softly to the men that have come in the SUVs, who offer them cold beer in the shade. They see the money wrapped in rubber bands and shake to the terms. The train engines restart, with a retching noise, and the smoke chokes and gathers, and the ticket lines remove their ropes, and a woman with drawn-on black brows, white eyeshadow, and a striped tube top underneath a navy jacket takes our credit card and says the time of arrival at Machu Picchu will be niy-een oh seben.

And then, we are in a small village tucked into the edge of the Andes and the jungle. There are masses of tourists, Germans looking at papers, Japanese, with well-tied shoes and small packs, Americans in ratty cargo pants and tanks. We are lined into buses that spiral up a long and typical winding South American road, the kind with no barriers overlooking huge ra-vines, the kind where you pile out at the end, crumpled and oily from nervous sweat, shaken and nauseous to the large mist-covered park they call Machu Picchu. First thing is, it looks exactly like the pictures you've seen everywhere. I wonder why we must visually rape everything. Nothing harbors mystery, as it must've in the ancient times, when the young explorer in 1911, Hiram Bingham, traipsed through noxious jungle and heavily breathing, lifted his stunned eyes to this place. Now groups of Japanese skitter like crabs, breathily whispering, hai, hai, and Germans laugh while holding up a Peru travel book as they are photographed over the grand peak. I start following one particularly flamboyant tour guide with odd speech patterns, and now, you please, peoples, please, for me to follow, I brings to you temple of the sun.

And yet, it is the very essence of beauty. Despite the swarmings of crowds and the overphotographed imagery, it lies quietly and demands respect.

As does love. You can parade it around, analyze it, destroy it with words and actions. You can ignore it with 401(k)s and daily life, and trips to the gym and watching CNN, and yet, like Machu Picchu, in the end, you stand stunned: there is no mystery greater or more complex, more inexplicable or confusing. It just is, and that is all. Just accept.

Incidentally, I did not see wild parrots, though I was amazed to see flocks of them near the bay in Rehoboth Beach, Delaware. Clusters of green birds on power lines, which on close examination, did indeed appear to be parrots. A local dispersed the history: a crate carrying the birds broke near the water, and they learned to acclimate.

❖ Ceviche

 1 pound red snapper fillets or any good-quality whitefish
  fillets, cut into 1-inch pieces
 1 medium onion, thinly sliced
 Salt and pepper to taste
 Pinch of cayenne pepper
 1 garlic clove, minced
 1 hot chile pepper, finely chopped
 3 tablespoons chopped fresh cilantro
 Juice of 3 lemons
 Juice of 3 sour oranges or limes

Place fish on a platter. Place onion slices on fish. Add remaining ingredients, covering with the juices. Refrigerate the ceviche at least 4 hours before serving.

Serve on a bed of lettuce and garnish with slices of cold sweet potato accompanied with hot corn on the cob.

Chapter 8

The Catsuit

New York City, 1990

At a Japanese restaurant where I worked in Washington, D.C., I met Russell, who had recently returned from a kibbutz in Israel. We married, moved to New York, and then, inexplicably, an old chum of my mother's from Smith College decided it was high time I joined the Junior League. Never mind that in those days I sported a favorite black catsuit perennially, along with thigh-high suede boots and a prerequisite thrift shop leopard coat. Along with this finery, my hair was bleached out à la Debbie Harry and I pretty much modeled my makeup after her, too—finger-thick eyeliner, and ketchup lips.

Perhaps she thought it was an unfortunate stage or maybe I had been decoupaged with her old memory of my mother from Smith, but regardless, she insisted I meet her and Charlie at the Junior League mansion, fashionably situated in the Upper East Side.

It was appropriately chintzed out, antiqued, and reserved in the old preppie way. Housed in an old mansion, it sported room after room of comfortable lounges. Russell balked all the way. I felt strange, yet I was drawn in by curiosity. At the front, a stationary display offered styles that could be purchased to support some homeless shelter, a sea of bright pink monograms and parrot green addresses that one could just snatch up right there and then. It was a good deal, helping the unfortunate while penning thank you notes about last night's gala.

Wearing the old catsuit (I don't think I owned anything else) but with a reserved black coat, I found Charlie and Nancy in the lounge. It was a field of Shetland sweaters in pastel and clean-cut Junior Leaguers, shiny, scrubbed, and drinking gallons of gin. There was lots of real liquor being served, not just the perennial Chardonnay, served with silver bowls of "those fabulous nuts" as Nancy called them. The only person of color that I could see was Johnny, the bartender, an old-timer in a white dinner coat. I knew his name was Johnny because just when we sat down, a lanky brunette rushed in clad in a fur coat.

"Johnny, darling, I need a scotch as fast as you can pour it. Pour one for Rodge, too, he's on his way."

And Johnny poured the amber fluid expertly, as always, smiling, and she just signed the bill, because cash was never, ever used at the Mansion.

At this time in our lives, my new husband and I lived in a fourth floor walk-up on St. Marks Place between 1st and A, pushing aside heroin dealers blasting dance-hall music in the doorway. A man would walk up and down our block dressed as a tree and another woman skittered by every day, her entire face covered with rags, hunkered down between her shoulders. The street was often smeared with vomit, dogshit, and spit. I was a painter, a waitress, and occasional caterer and my husband worked at an alternative video store.

For one weird moment, after the woman ordered the drinks with her imperious air, I kind of floated on some strange fantasy world. The whole mansion was so cushioned from the ugly realities of life, acting as if money were no problem and race relations were irrelevant, and that life was polished, glamorous, and old-fashioned. It, in fact, seemed timeless. Like I was observing the world of my stylish grandparents, who went to Princeton and deb balls and yacht clubs, and their life wasn't a question but an answer. I could probably slide in, change my clothes a bit (a lot), and go for a ride for a while. Just push nasty old art to the side and worry about stationery and parties and, oh, where to go this summer. But, I got back to reality somewhere in the midst of crunching on those almonds and Nancy saying I just needed three references to get in, and then wouldn't it be just so much fun?

We left the mansion with appropriate warm goodbyes and Nancy kept calling. She had me cater a cocktail party for her, but then she didn't call again. Either she had realized the Junior League would rather throw up than have some vagabond like me in their midst or she found out my catering partner had snitched some wine and accidently burned a linen napkin (I actually showed her the napkin, but she wasn't pleased because her grandmother had given it to her). So we just stayed in our little downtown scene most of the time, and then when we had kids, decided we were too old and square for the East Village so we moved out to Park Slope and got a backyard and an electric grill.

New York has so many different worlds coexisting, spinning around each other, never touching, seemingly lost in time and space, me in my catsuit in the village, some pseudo beatnik, and the Junior League, in pearls, untouched and dining well. Sometimes we think that what we could have been stays with us, a possibility that can be whipped out if every thing else goes bad. As if all of our opportunities are not chances but layers of ourselves that are temporarily put away. And yet, my Junior League self never was and never would be, she stays angry and bitter, an aborted fetus, pissed for the Tiffany boxes that'll never be opened with her hands, hungry for the scotch and barbecued nuts that Johnny puts out each evening. As I live in the East Village in my catsuit, eating pierogis in the Polish delis, painting, catering and then, pushing a leopard-toned stroller, she crouches in the corner, her hair bobbed and clean, waiting.

About the same time, I developed a case of hives that kept coming and going, driving me to desperate oatmeal baths and carrying Benadryl everywhere I went. Plus, I also wore the catsuit everywhere and had to shimmy my hand under the fabric in contortions to reach the itchy spots. In desperation, I walked into a storefront Chinese herbalist on the way to Triple Eight Palace to eat dim sum on Canal Street. It was a narrow little spot, lined with glass shelves full of odd roots and seeds and a small, oily lady with a pockmarked face who inquired if she could help us. I explained my problem and she led me to the back, a dirty examining room shared with other patients. The doctor was in his sixties and had the worst breath I'd ever encountered, hot and algaic. He took my pulse and looked at my tongue. He gave me a bag of smelly herbs to brew into a tea and sent me off. I was to see him again in a week.

In a week, I'd improved but had a bad outbreak the day I saw him.

"Show me them," he said.

I panicked. I was wearing a very sleazy black thong and a black push-up bra, plus thigh-high boots.

"No need to take those off" he said, pointing to the boots. "Just pull down clothes."

Terrified and red, yet desperate to get rid of my hives, I peeled the suit down to my thighs and lay there, feeling like a specimen as he probed my stomach.

"You feel hot, cold?"

He had me flip over—quite awkward—and exclaimed, "You all sweaty!" because I was damp from lying on the metal table (no tissue like Western doctors) and nerves.

Horrible scenarios ran through my head, bad encounters with the doctor, and then trying to explain what happened to some tough NYC cop from the Bronx.

"So you say this guy molested you?"

"Yes, officer. Here in this office."

"What were you doing?"

"Well, I was lying down on this examining table with my catsuit pulled down to my thigh-high boots (suede with three-inch heels), exposing my naked buttocks in a fio dental Brazilian thong and this push-up bra, all sweaty, you know, a typical doctor-patient thing."

"Why didn't you put on a gown?"

"Ah, well."

"Did you even ask for a license? And he treated you with a bag of dried roots?"

But the hives went away. He also got rid of my husband's plantar warts, which he had tried to do for years, to no avail.

• • •

Catsuits will make a comeback, no doubt. I won't be wearing them, though, since I'm older and heavier and it takes a certain youthful panache. Around this time, I really did nothing. I had waitressed for years, attempting to claim my right as a painter, though I rarely painted. I was trying to become a caterer. I worked for a small caterer in Tribeca and walked five flights of stairs everyday to chop onions and peel leaves from watercress stems. The company was run a by a nice gay man in the village and yes, anything went. We sat at a wooden table slicing crudités and cracking jokes all day long. After that, I applied for a really professional position in a posh caterer where they all wore real chef suits. The main chef interviewed me and asked me sharp, probing questions: What is déglacé? What is meringue? It was all so bizarre, and luckily since I had studied all those old yellowed cookbooks of Golly's, I knew all his silly answers. I wore the white chef jacket and showed up.

It was a bit more challenging than Anything Goes! No, this time I had to really cook. First, I had to make real mayonnaise. I knew the components, in fact I'd done it many a time. But of course, for some reason, it didn't work, sloshing in the blender like bright yellow paint. It wouldn't emulsify, I think the eggs were too cold. I tried to pour it down the sink secretly, but I could see the sharp little glances from the Thai girl and the American guy in their perfect CIA coats and clogs. No doubt they knew I was a poseur, I didn't even have my own set of knives! All the real chefs carry their knives in a soft cloth portfolio and they wear proper kitchen shoes. I was probably wearing the old catsuit. I had one good knife at home, a nicked sashimi knife, but no cloth portfolio. Should I brandish it in my hand as I take the subway? After the mayonnaise disaster, I had to make endless phyllo purses. He said, invent some lamb filling with apricots, which I did with ease, flavoring it with Moroccan spices. Then, he said, make three hundred langues de chats. All chefs fall into two categories, those that bake and those that cook. Baking is a precise science, and takes a very specific personality, exacting and careful. Plus, delicate and cool hands help with the preparation of pastry. The other form of chef is an artist, inventor, more involved in creation and taste than perfect measurements. Now, during the interview, I specifically stated, I do not bake. I repeated that, though in a weak and faltering voice, because it was obvious from his pinched face, there would be no choice, my job was on the line, etc. I followed the recipe to a T: langues de chats, meaning cat's tongues, a crisp French tea cookie made with egg whites, sugar, and flour, piped on parchment paper and baked for eleven minutes. No problem.

Unfortunately, I didn't know jack about convection ovens, which seem to contain a hidden wind tunnel. As soon as I placed the cookie pans inside the paper flew up and plastered the dough to the sides of the hot oven, which started sizzling and burning. I tried quietly to put out the flames, but the alarmed crew, the Thai chef, the American including the irate cake lady who worked there, ran over to assist, their attitude condescending and snippy. At this point, I retreated to a corner to cut crudités, chagrined.

I finally found a job as a waitress in a small trattoria on 1st Avenue, and I mean small, there were probably ten tables, run by the grumpiest old Italian man in the world named Tony. He was small and compact, a bright red face crumpled like a fist. He'd yell at you for anything, if you threw away a half-eaten piece of bread (we use it) or if the cook peeled an onion too much (a waste). He yelled when I sat, when I walked, when I spoke. I basically just kept on the move. The manager was his poor son-in-law, Donnie, who had crushed several discs in his spine, but hobbled around just the same and Tony yelled at him, too. Donnie and I moved like watery martyrs through the tepid angry sea of Tony, in some codependent relationship of hell. Tony had a flamboyant redheaded girlfriend who came through occasionally, with smeared lipstick spreading on her cracked lips and a tangle of plastic bright baubles around her wrists. Give her what she wants, he'd growl. And she'd drink rosé, and eat beef straciole.

They sold spleen sandwiches with ricotta (re-got) on small soft rolls, that was their thing. These little babies were called vastedda (pronounced vash-ted) and Tony would first lubricate a few pieces of spleen in a large hot vat of lard, place it in a soft bun with sliced ricotta and some Parmesan. It wasn't bad, but it was an acquired taste, similar to chewy liver. Limos and Mercedes would pull up front to order piles and piles of spleen sandwiches to go. They'd place them in paper bags with grease spots and tan women with huge French-nailed hands and tight jeans would take them away. At lunch the tables would fill up with plumbers from Staten Island or electricians from Brooklyn, young guys with big boots and hair as wet and slick as seals. These guys had a rough style I liked, they ordered too much, they laughed too much, and in the end, they fought for the bill and ended up just throwing cash all over the table in small, crumpled wads. As opposed to the small Italian lady named Pearl who came for her peas and maca-rone soup, and always left a pile of pennies and nickels.

But Tony could cook. Who said good cooks have to be jolly.

The Catsuit

Cranky old Tony made the best rice balls, arancini (aran-
cheen). Fluffy balls of mushy rice, rolled around a small inner
section of peas and ground meat, rolled in bread crumbs, and
served with marinara. And he taught me how to peel broccoli
rabe stems and then sauté the greens and stems in garlic and
oil. I liked their lentil soup, a simple affair made just with
water, carrots, and greens, then drizzled with olive oil and
Parmesan.

My last day with Tony came unexpectedly. One day my husband came in for lunch and suddenly Tony railed off on some
minute mistake I had made, screaming about sauce, and in a
nanosecond my husband was up in his face, all of his 160 pounds
on his skinny frame.

Don't yell at my wife.

I'll do whatever the hell I want. Tony was tough.

Not at my *wife*.

Get the hell outa here.

There were screams and threats. The customers stared.

My husband grabbed my hand. We left. Unfortunately, I
had left my apron there full of money, so I came back in a
hour.

You looking for this, he said, holding it out.

Yes.

Listen. You're a bootiful person. You're a bootiful girl. But
your husband, he don't come here no more.

I looked at his small, boiled face. I actually realized he liked
me then.

Hey Tony. You got a vash-ted goin for me? A man blocking
the sun of the door said, a large Lincoln double-parked with a
ragged bleach blond hanging out the side.

Ay. Sure thing.

Feed the Hungry

I grabbed the apron and took out the money.

You leave that apron, hear?

I said nothing. I hardly wanted the half-poly apron covered in spaghetti sauce and anchovy oil.

I passed the vash-ted guy and came out on 1st Avenue.

I needed comfort.

I ducked into a Polish take-out I liked one door down. They only had two refrigerators in a space cool and dark like a closet. They sold homemade pierogis (peer-oges). They sold a cold borscht in plastic quart tubs, sour and creamy, a high fuchsian tub of beets and dill. I bought one, went home, counted my change. For a while and for reasons unknown, I missed Tony and Donnie and Siciliana. I'd walk by and see the cars double parked and wish I could walk in, but again, that door had closed.

I got pregnant after that. One day, my mother was visiting from Virginia and had made a favorite comfy meal: roast chicken with gravy, mashed potatoes, mozzarella and tomato salad, I ate a lot, and was relaxing when a backache came upon me and it got worse and worse. By eleven, my mother and Russell knew something was wrong: I was only all fours, moaning and yelling. An ambulance came, we rushed to Columbia-Presbyterian Hospital on 186th Street. At 2:26 A.M. I gave birth. The only problem was that he was only six months old, weighing in at 2.2 pounds.

Ivan was the size of a beer bottle, a shrill tiny thing, looking like a skinned rabbit, not the heavy pink-faced bundles I saw in the maternity ward. He had tubes in every direction, poking him, drawing blood every hour, a plastic mask taped to his face. They didn't even know what caused it, but of course I was filled with guilt: had I worked too much? Stressed too much? Not eaten properly? (After my next son, we discovered my uterus was heart-shaped, and therefore couldn't hold to full term.) That night they only gave him a ten-percent chance of survival. For the next three months I sat in Columbia-Presbyterian Hospital next to him. My only stress relief was food, and I got larger and larger. I'd go down to the cafeteria, where they had Caribbean food on certain days. Or, in the neighborhood, the Dominican restaurants were good, I'd have boiled cassava, pork, rice and beans, and waddle back to stay by Ivan. I remember vividly the stress of taking the elevator up to the sixth floor. Every minute upward would escalate in stress, and as I emerged and went down the hall, I would subtly translate any nuance in the atmosphere: if the doctor would look slightly distant, I'd panic and think Ivan was dying, or if a nurse scurried by, I'd assume Ivan was in distress. On a daily basis, they'd test his lungs or his eyes or his intestines. Babies around us died or suffered brain bleeds, but Ivan just kept on, sleeping, occasionally screeching. Finally, after three months, we cautiously brought him home, all four pounds of him, and he somehow, miraculously grew normally. At fifteen, these days are so long ago, he ranges around in ragged jeans with an iPod attached to his ear, his hair a mop.

The stress of New York was getting to me. It took too long to get a taxi and carrying a stroller on and off the subway was getting old. It took hours to simply grocery shop. My backyard was rough and sooty. Spring came and went with hardly a speck of green and I missed Virginia and the ease of it all. We moved back.

I notice Siciliana closed. Word has it it reopened further downtown and now is half Mexican.

❖ Cold Borscht

3 medium beets
2½ quarts water
Salt
Juice of 1 lemon
3 medium all-purpose potatoes, such as Yukon Gold, boiled then peeled
8 hard-boiled eggs
2 cucumbers
Sour cream
Fresh dill

Add beets to water in a large pot and bring to boil. Cook until done, about 45 minutes. Add salt to taste. Remove pot from stove to cool.

When beets are cool enough to handle, coarsely grate and return to water. Add lemon juice. Chill in refrigerator overnight. On the next day, coarsely chop potatoes, eggs, and cucumbers, and add to a soup. Add sour cream and dill and serve.

❖ Arancini

Filling
½ pound ground chuck
½ cup extra virgin olive oil
½ teaspoon garlic powder
Salt and pepper

The Catsuit

½ cup tomato sauce
1 cup peas (fresh or frozen)
1 cup grated Parmesan cheese
4 eggs, separated
4 cups cooked rice
2 cups Italian flavored bread crumbs
1½ cups vegetable oil for frying finished product

Sauté meat in 2 tablespoons olive oil, breaking up well. Add garlic powder, salt and pepper to taste, ¼ cup of the tomato sauce, and peas. Simmer gently for about 10 minutes. Allow mixture to cool. Meanwhile, add cheese and egg yolks to rice. Add remaining tomato sauce a little at a time to rice, just enough to add a little color. Mix well. Shape into balls about the size of a small orange. Poke hole in center and insert about 1 teaspoon of filling. Pat balls with unbeaten egg white, then roll in bread crumbs. Heat oil in deep frying pan and gently fry balls to a golden color. Drain on paper towels.

Chapter 9

Greenwood

My Family's Attempt at Culinary Coup,
Christmas Eve

During the years in Harbour Island the whole family was together: Harrison, Owen, Nancy, Gene, John and I, Moira, sometimes her sister, Shelley, and then, John Daniel. In Almond Tree, Christmas Eve was celebrated with a stuffed crawfish made by the cranky Carrie, who used too much pepper. We children would sleep up in the attic, and I swore one Christmas I heard bells on the roof. The air smelled of jasmine and rotten fruit, like it always did, and the adults were all downstairs drinking rum. Joe Petty made coconut candy for us children, roughly hewn squares in bright pink, like my Nancy's Lilly dresses. There are smells floating up from the house now as I speak, wafts of some other time as clear as a moment ago—a soapy, sour fruity smell by the stairs, a whiny cedar smell from the living room built-in cabinets, whose doors stuck, and where we housed games. This smell you will know if you've ever gone to camp in New England, it's the same resiny whiff you get in the barracks, or when you come to open up an old vacation home. New houses never have this smell, this faint waft of yesteryear.

We'd pilfer a ragged tree from the beach, almost needleless, but it would do. We dragged ham in our suitcases from Virginia. Presents also had to be packed and brought, in fact it was all a giant hassle, until you came in the squeaking front screen door, came in from the tropical front yard, where we'd pick those soldier crabs, and smelled that crawfish all high with sherry and pepper in your face, kissed your grandfather fragrant with lime and grandmother of Dior and saw your stockings lumpy and full lying on the fireplace, and then you wondered who could live without an island Christmas. Those days are gone. That family is dissipated and flung throughout the world—Nancy in her cottage in the home in Charlottesville, Harrison on his ranch in Montana, Ann and John Daniel in Greenwood, Moira dead, Gene dead, Owen in an asylum. Harbour Island was one of those fragile threads that came and went.

But we still carry on in Greenwood. Sometime around May, I start thinking about Christmas Eve. I am not one of those permanent Christmas types, who hoard lights and ornaments bought half-price the day after Christmas. No, I am talking about the food, of course. We go all out, as people in Virginia say. We hunker down into some form of bestial gluttony, winging money around for rare items like sea urchin in the shell or white truffles. Sitting in a cavernous stone room and washing it all down with champagne and then going home, glutted and nauseated, ready for a early morning quaff of more champagne and leftover cheese from the night before. We are a family that has no 401(k)s, no stocks, no mutual funds. There are no college funds of Keogh accounts. We are simple hedonists, people living day to day, usually for the enjoyment of some idle food treat. We don't have boats or mountain bikes or expensive cars. We have edible trifles. And Christmas Eve represents the ultimate burning of the potlatch, the pièce de resistance for the foodie wastrels that we are.

For a couple of years now, I've silently tried to compose a toast to Jesus Christ, something interesting, esoteric, something remarkable about the man, like "did anyone know Christ collected small Eritrean coins?" but I can't find any information like this, and I'm afraid to cross that nebulous line and ruin the evening by announcing to everyone, "I'd like to talk about Jesus!" and watch the glassy eyes of my family and friends turning pallidly from their snapper en croûte to stare at my new evangelist self. But I think about it a lot, that all this gluttony should have some reference to the actual event that supposedly we are celebrating. As far as we get is, did you know that the animals talk at midnight? We really love that one, for about two seconds. Then it's back to course number fourteen.

The whole event has taken years to morph into as what it is now: a smorgasbord of outrageous hors d'ouevres washed down in globules of champagne, then grappa. We're up for a variation at this point, but we've settled into a groove. Oh, we tried the seated deal. One year I ordered a full rack of lamb, back before these were readily available in mass markets, shrink-wrapped, like transistor radios from Japan. The bones were untrimmed, covered in Crazy Glue fat, and they were about six feet long, so they had to be trimmed, i.e., sawed off, and my kitchen tools in those days consisted of one butter knife and a broken wine key. I actually did spend quite some time with a stainless steel steak knife heaving back and forth against one bone, covered in sheep fat, which not only refuses to wash off your hands but also comes back in hefty, musky wafts as you wear your Christmas mohair sweater later overlaid with a sickly sweet perfume (a horrific combo, sheep fat and mohair: one could describe a perfume as such: Afghani Nights).

Finally I broke down and drove to my stepfather's sculpture studio, a massive lean-to of fiberglass and every tool ever created, provided it's fifty years old and makes a spray of green, sulfurous sparks. We roughly hewed them down (it got a bit out of control, it knocked the bones down quickly and a bit too short). Covering them with the traditional persillade masked some of the flesh-burning odor. You can't imagine the smoke a rack of lamb, or this one at least, created, due to the ever-cantankerous wick of this ancient fat. Sheep fat is strong and solid, crumbly. Persian lambs have large chunks in their tails, which is threaded between hunks of meat on kebabs and keeps them amply moistened during grilling. The kitchen abruptly filled with smoke, and then I had to slice the rack quickly before the fat hardened into that mouth-coating musk-filled lard, so suffice it to say, I was quite pro the appetizer selection idea once it surfaced. I think each and every one of us had experienced the solitary Siberia of the kitchen while others champagned in the living room and grew to resent it.

By the way, I use the term living room lightly, playfully, because my parents, the original Luddites, live in a house that appears to be transported from a fourteenth-century Irish village, minus the modern conveniences villagers enjoyed in those days, like warmth. The living room is a huge stone rectangle with one big hearth, and what I'm getting around to say is: it's cold as hell. it takes two days to heat up, with various portable heaters plugged in to fill in the gaps. The aforementioned rack of lamb instantly congealed to a gummy layer of fat within a nanosecond of entering the room, whereupon the silver platter became frozen, and let's just say the mouth feel of the lamb was not exactly pleasant, unless you like lanolin as a foodspread. All food in that room instantly freezes. It's a bit of a problem. There was one odd Christmas Eve with three random Italians, okay, I dated one of them and okay, he was fifty and he came with his son, but we didn't know the other one. We all wore coats and frost came out of our mouths and we drank copious amounts of grappa to compensate for the blackening of our extremities. I think that was the lowest point, we've managed to shed outer-wear since then.

So, around May, or actually, truth be told, even sometimes on December 26, we begin the what-I'm-going-to-make musing. A good segment of the night is this long verbal foreplay we seem to create throughout the year: I'm doing foie gras this year. I'm flying in oysters and rockefellerizing them. The ahead planning is crucial for developing the appetite, and actually creating momentum, since the advent of my children, I am usually lucky to even be able to put on clothes on that day. How I managed before to buy presents, wrap them, decorate a house, do stockings, bake a gingerbread house, and devein a foie gras in years back I have no idea. These days on Christmas Eve I have the energy that even opening a can of beans would be a bit too much. So, through the years, I've learned a trick from ca-tering: buy something flashy, delicious that takes zero prep work. For years, while I lived in Manhattan, that would trans-late as caviar, which by the way, is my all-time favorite food. As a child, my special birthday treat was cheap store-bought caviar (the kind that is the size of mustard seeds, drowned in ink, in a small glass jar in the "gourmet" section of the supermarket, next to canned snails and powdered Knorr hollandaise). this was served with a dollop of sour cream on Devonsheer melba toast rounds. I also responded heartily to the wonderful "caviar pie" my grandparents would occasionally proffer at dinner parties, layers of cream cheese, caviar, chopped eggs, green onions, served with crackers.

But I had matured and required the real thing: beluga. The caviar I bought in a small dark stall in the Fulton fish market at five A.M. from a gruff old Russian man who sat on a stool, listening to the radio. I would emerge from my house, while the streets were dark blue and the early purveyor trucks barreled down 1st Avenue, teddy bears tied to their bumpers, and take a taxi down to the waterfront. Old rusty barrels in the streets burned with fires, and I usually wore an all-encompassing long suede coat, my blond hair tucked under a cap, because otherwise, being the only woman in the midst of these fishmongers, I would be whistled at and hassled nonstop. It was a man's world, for sure, but pearlishly feminine in its guise—the fish glistened on piles of ice like moonstones, all sorts of shellfish squirmed and rattled. Everything was jewelishly bright, stellar almost, and the smell was the sharp salute of the sea. The meat market of Gansevoort is the masculine world, with its haunches of purplish and green flesh, the hummed down reek of blood. It was lonely at the fish market, like everything about the sea. When fishing, the mythical image is solitude, silence, a lone man in a boat out in the wilds of the sea. The market felt the same, the cold dark street, burning fires, the glistening fish. I would twist and turn in alleys until I came to the Russian. He didn't say much. A handwritten note on a scrap of cardboard offered beluga, osetra, Caspian Sea. This was before the embargo. I'd buy a nice wallop and then meander back, clutching the tiny jewels. I didn't do anything to them, just dollop on plain toast. On the side, there was crème fraîche, chopped egg, lemon, for those who wish to adulter the taste, but I like it pure, popping like beads in the mouth.

Years later, after I left New York and moved back to Virginia, my son, Sunny's, first delight as a toddler was salmon roe. He'd order it in the Japanese steakhouses we'd take him to for a few peaceful minutes of dining, never mind that the chef was Korean, with incorrect rice, badly hewn fish, who cared. We were in Virginia then, and sushi was basically a hijacked thing everywhere, unless we went to D.C. And peace of mind during dinner had become tantamount. He would bite off the caviar roof of the sushi. He called them "orange peas."

Once I was lucky to find a trove of diver scallops with the roe in the shell, which I brought down from New York for the Virginia Christmas Eve fete. I broiled them briefly, tossed a tiny dash of butter on top, and served.

My parents' standbys for years were white truffles that they would order through Balducci's, but the last couple of years they've been unsatisfactory, so now we have their famous hand-gathered morels from our woods, cooked in cream in simple puff pastry. My mother usually makes a soft smoked salmon roll, injected with a delicate mousse. The prerequisite oysters are shipped in from Maine, briny and cold. We favored the belon but then my brother John cleverly persuaded us to shift to the bluepoints. Other than those classics, we shift and migrate between whatever we have salivated over and mused through the year, and what shows up fresh and sumptuous. The highlight perhaps is John's famous smoked venison tenderloin. This is coming from someone who hates venison. Years of living with my parents brought lots of venison to the table.

Haunches, sausage, stews, roasts. Always with the characteristic musty flavor I abhor. Then a brief romance with a country boy who liked to hunt when I was eighteen brought an even worse rash of venison horrors—venison chili, venison stews made with canned potatoes, unseasoned venison fried in a pan. He and his friends, who worked in construction, spent the weekends in a small rambler in West Virginia, where we drank beer, listened to Little Feat, and ate venison. The only lights in the house were fluorescent bars in the ceilings, the walls were covered in paneling, the floors were cheaply carpeted, the furniture was man-style early seventies pioneer plaid. Definitely the least aesthetically sensitive time of my life. I was taking a year off before going to Bennington and I was really underground. I worked as a waitress in a colonial restaurant and had to wear a full-length southern belle hooped dress to serve people ancient foods of yore. I really hated his venison chili. I would instead go up the hill to a diner called Cindy Lou's, which offered a great chili topped with French fries.

But my brother's venison is actually fantastic. First of all, he knows how to hunt well and he slaughters the deer himself, being careful to cut off the musk glands immediately, which causes the musty flavor I dislike. Then, being a chef by trade, he knows to age the meat in cold air for a while, which tenderizes it. Then, he takes the tenderloin and smokes it in his fireplace with walnut wood. What he produces is thinly sliced, very lean, rare and succulent. It disappears rapidly.

As I said, we used to spend Christmas in Harbour Island, Bahamas, before the family fell apart over the years, slowly and raggedly, like the blanket a toddler yanks around, a piece here, a nugget there, until finally you are left with a small, tattered scrap, cherished. In those days, we stuffed ourselves on local fare, sweet crawfish and grouper, conch and rum. We fantasize about renting a house there again. I am thinking about stuffed crawfish this year, a surprise. But lately, I've abandoned the hors d'oeuvres. I bring a hot casserole of khoresht bademjoon, since I am in my Persian stage. A rich stew of eggplant, lamb, saffron, unripened grapes, served with perfumey basmati rice, most people can't resist a spoonful or two in the cold room, full of cheer, champagne, laughter, a large fire.

The old Labs lie in wait under the table, lapping up the odd crust of foie gras or venison morsel, waiting for their moment of verbal freedom. Once Leaner, a black Lab, snuck in the kitchen and ate an entire twelve-inch pâté loaf, which was on a silver platter waiting to be served. My brother and I heard the loud *goddddddamnit* of my stepfather, and instantly intuiting the situation, we bet over which pâté went down, the mushroom or the foie gras.

❖ John's Famous Smoked Venison with Horseradish Sauce

¼ cup quatre épices
2 teaspoons crushed dried juniper berries
2 teaspoons dried thyme
Salt and pepper to taste

1 whole loin of venison (2 pounds beef can be substituted;
    any size is fine, though smaller would tend to work
    better)
Horseradish sauce (see below)

Mix seasonings and use them to thickly coat tenderloin. Place tenderloin overnight in refrigerator, uncovered, to dry slightly. The next day, place venison either in a smoker on very low or hang directly from a hook in a woodstove, with a pan underneath. Allow only a very low flame with smoldering coals. Wood is best. Allow the loin to smoke for 3 hours.

    Cool venison. Slice very thin and serve with horseradish sauce.

❖ Horseradish Sauce

One 4-ounce jar premium white horseradish
One 8-ounce container sour cream
Salt and pepper to taste

Mix all ingredients together and serve.

❖ Morels and Cream

1 cup heavy cream
3 tablespoons unsalted butter
1 pound fresh morels, trimmed, washed well, and patted dry
1 tablespoon all-purpose flour
Salt
Freshly ground white pepper
5 thin slices brioche or challah bread, crusts trimmed, each
    slice cut into 4 triangles and toasted

Heat cream in a small saucepan until hot.
    Heat butter in 12-inch heavy skillet over moderately high heat

until foam subsides, then sauté morels in the butter, stirring frequently, until golden, 6 to 8 minutes. Sprinkle in flour and cook, stirring, 1 minute. Stir in hot cream and reduce heat to low. Gently simmer, covered, stirring once, until morels are tender, 10 to 15 minutes. Season with salt and white pepper.

Arrange five toasts on each of four plates and spoon morels and sauce on top. Serve immediately.

Chapter 10

The Insanity of the Servitude Industry

1980–1990

Ihave worked in every kind of restaurant under the sun under the pretense somehow that I was "a painter," when most days I actually just lay around recuperating from waiting tables. I probably produced fifteen paintings in ten years and just one group show. I was intensely unambitious, probably because my stepfather was an artist, my father was an artist, and I did such different stuff I felt intimidated.

My first job, at age eighteen, was at a restaurant in Warrenton, Virginia, a small pizza deli run by two Palestinian brothers. I worked together with the older one: I would take orders, fold pizza boxes, and he would cook. Unfortunately, he also liked to corner me in the back as I went to gather more napkins, singing my name in a strange Middle-Eastern lilt, naaaaannnneeeeeee-eee, but it didn't do much for me, I'd say, you have a wife, and he did and several kids, but this was pooh-poohed off with the old "you can't eat filet mignon every day" line. There was a group of regulars that came in, old retired blue collar types, kind men, and I spent much time talking to them. When I left for college, the group of old men chipped in and bought me a bracelet in a velvet box.

A few years later, after a brief and unsuccessful stint at Bennington College, I left and came to Washington. My grandfather, Francis, offered me his small hideaway in a brownstone that he owned near the zoo and I gladly accepted. It was a dark and unfinished basement, covered in dust. There was a cot, a disheveled mini kitchen, a huge hole in the wall, and many somber Catholic reminders—crosses, icons. The cot was foldable metal, covered in a dingy orange polyester blanket. The only window looked blearily out into the alley. I took a job in a jazz café across the street, a small place run by a woman named Zena and her three children. She was unkind, shrill, and in fact, insane. I cowered around her most days. The famous dish of Park Place was "pizza in a dish," all the toppings of pizza melted in the microwave in a glass bowl. The chef was the son, and nobody knew the business. There was no planning, food was never ordered. We ran out of everything. Across the road lay the Sheraton and we would be thronged by hordes of conventioneers. Long lines would pour out the front and I would have to handle a crowd of a hundred alone. But we would seat them, give them menus. They would stare vacantly and urgently as I came into the dining room, looking for the pizza in a dish. Coins and dollars were flung on tables as people left in disgust. It was high stress.

Next door was the posh and elegant Pettitos, run by two Italian brothers. This was top service, the waiters wore long aprons, crisp white shirts. They ground pepper, popped open wine, tossed Caesar salads at the table. At the Park Place café, we were lucky to slide a grilled cheese sloppily across the cloth as we ran down the worn stairs to get table number seven's order. Most days, my hair was matted greasily to my forehead, my shirt stained. Our plates contained piles of road waste, while Pettitos offered real northern Italian food, which in the eighties was considered refined and nouvelle: white sauces, veal, mozzarella and tomato salad, the American palate didn't know these, having been brought up on "macaroni and gravy." I handled the outdoor patio at Park Place, while Ben handled the patio at Pettitos, polished and sleek in his long apron and gleaming black hair. He was from New York and snapped his fingers for busboys, his sooty hair never out of place. Later on I knew he used a gel called "shpritz forte." "He would also say he was "shvitzing like a mother." When I was slammed and in the weeds, as we say in the restaurant business, Ben twirled and peppered and suavely tossed a lettuce leaf. He also asked me out several times a night. I always said no, but he persisted. He always ended his fast, staccato sentences with youknowthatdon'tyou. He was Jewish and called me his "shiksa goddess," and I refused his advances. He persisted. He said, you're going to have dinner with me tomorrow youknowthatdon'tyou. After a while, I just got weary.

He took me to a small French restaurant in Georgetown, plied me with Frangelico, took me to a club called Numbers. I had never done any of this. I lived in an odd broken-down cave, and come to think of it, always had. I had a handful of clothes. I must have seemed bohemian, simply because I could only afford old thrift shop dresses. I worked in a nursing home in college down the street from Bennington, and I actually had to go to the Salvation Army and steal a nurse's outfit because I couldn't afford one. Ben lived in a sleek apartment, one of those grand and huge complexes with many towers, east and west.

His furniture was new, chrome and black leather, which he rented. His closet was perfectly organized, I didn't have one, I lived out of a suitcase. He had a pristine white BMW, I walked.

Ben cooked dinner for me, steak, shrimp, and Rice-A-Roni. He sang "Volare" out of tune. We became a couple. He liked me to wear perfect red polished toes and fingers, immaculate makeup, and pointy stiletto shoes. He gave me furs and gold. He saw my broken cave and immediately packed all my items—my suitcase—into a box and brought me to the apartment. I had little objection, I was a drifter. He set up my small toilette in a corner and was amused by my odd ways. For example, I became obsessed with Indian food, buying bags and bags of spices at Indian Appliances and Spices in Arlington. I had asafetida, garam masala, fresh turmeric root. I made dal, rotis, sambar, endless chutneys, all to his disdain. You makin that fuckin stinky shit again, he'd say, laughing, when he'd come home to his previously immaculate apartment that before had always smelled cold and metallic like an industrial air conditioner. Now, he walked cautiously into a hall of fumes, cloudy with the stench of a cheap Bombay streetmonger's tent.

Turmeric stained his Formica and lamb burned and splattered in his white oven. But he didn't care. He was more interested in sitting on the couch. We would go up to New Jersey and visit his "ma" as he called her. She lived in a giant column of tinted glass just over the George Washington Bridge. We were greeted by her old doorman (hey Benny boy) and sat in an elevator for what seemed to be centuries. Finally we emerged to a handsome woman with short salt and pepper hair and red nails. The apartment was a cluster of plants and again, chrome and black leather furniture. She was dry and choppy, she worked in the "schmattas" business, the garment district, and I felt distinctly slow next to her. We stayed with "ma" and we'd go to dinner to Italian restaurants that knew "Elaine and Bennie," overly rococo places where the waiters had long sideburns and reeked of cheap cologne. They'd toss Caesar at the table and flame steak Diane. We'd have noodles and cannoles, as they called them. The next day we'd sleep in, then we'd go into "the city." Ben liked sautéed spinach in Little Italy at Mario's. Then, a course of veal piccata with angel hair puttanesca. I had never had any of this, but this was his metier. When we left, Elaine would sob in his arms. She'd pinch his cheeks, muss his hair.

When I moved to Ben's apartment, I worked in the cocktail lounge of The Watergate Hotel. It was a sort of velveteen brown pit in the bowels of the hotel. Most of the time it was pitifully empty, and just myself and a bartender named Reza stood guard. At ten, the Kennedy Center's theater emptied and they all seemed to flow into our lounge, a huge mass of crumpled tuxedos and dinner dresses demanding brandy and Irish coffees. Reza and I flew around like birds, tripping on the carpet, collapsing in a heap after they just as suddenly left. Reza was my age, fantastically handsome, the first Persian I ever knew. He invited me to dinner at his house. We drove to a huge high-rise in Arlington and sat uncomfortably as everyone babbled in Farsi, the young people around the TV, the older people sitting stiffly on couches. One old wizened gentleman offered me a nut. I am sure they wondered who I was. Politely, Reza brought me home, offering his hand for a shake at the end.

After The Watergate, I tried La Lumiese, a snug little French restaurant in Georgetown, where you had to wear an Alsatian peasant dress with a tie-up bodice. It was run, quite expertly I must add, by a watery-looking gentleman named Monsieur Pain, which sounds worse in English than in French. Because I sported a ragged dutchboy at this time, he called me "Cabbage-Patch doll." The employee meals were civilized affairs, with wine, salad, bread, eaten in leisure. There was a caustic gay man named Martin ("I only like ugly men," he said, "not handsome"), the voluptuous, mincing hostess, who actively and unabashedly pursued a rich husband, using the source of regulars as her pool, and the tiny sardonic doll named Margaux, wife of the severe and cold Laurent, who was the manager. Margaux looked twelve, but I believe she was in her thirties. She wore furs, Cartier jewelry, Cartier Must perfume. She had Louis Vuitton bags, Gucci clothes, all on her waitress's budget. And strangely, they were always accompanied by a beautiful young French boy named Frederic, about twenty-two. No one knew what his role was, but it seemed more than a friend, there was a secretive and passionate edginess to Margaux and Frederic, and Laurent seemed to care less.

The voluptuous, mincing hostess had targeted Monsieur Deveraux as her future husband. He came in daily, red faced, with a large bush of silken white hair, he would proceed to down three Bloody Marys before his couscous had even arrived. Unfortunately, Monsieur Deveraux would call me over, inquire about my life, begging me to go to Epcot Center with him. Like Hannibal Lecter, he told me, I tried human flesh once while in the Congo. It was in a stew, and rather tasty, as he drank a third Courvoisier. Sylvie was possessive, she would shoosh me away with a high-pitched shriek, you have tables! There was also the unfortunate Vito, a young blond Spaniard, who was the best waiter, professional and zippy, he could handle the whole room in a split second, traipsing down to the wine cellar, grasping three bottles of wine, spinning them open in seconds (unlike me, the cork in chunks on the table, red faced), pulling out huge trays in the kitchen on both hands, with perfect balance, always the long folded napkin, flapped out to deliver the dish. Vito was young, with a bevy of children already, but night after night he went out till all hours, and the sweatiness started, the speedy jitteriness. ("It is drug," said Margaux, "ah, idiot.") Sometimes, the tiny boss of us all, Margaux, cornered him by the bread ("You are very foolish boy, Vito") but of course, he ignored her, until the day he disappeared. Laurent called, there was lots of whispered French between them, and we never saw him again, nor did they divulge the details.

But, like soldiers, we obediently returned to the business at hand, simply caring for our six tables, a nightly gamble. Would they be kindly and patient, with good taste? Or would they be picky Americans who demanded the sauce stripped of every dish, the wine sent back, finally leaving a nine percent tip? At this point, Ben had finished his studies and was preparing to enter management. The relationship had dulled and was on its way out. He wanted to return to New York, with me. I longed for something else. Ben went back to New York and became a stockbroker. I fell in love with a Brazilian and moved to Brazil. Ben made me give back the fur coat, which I couldn't use in Brazil anyway.

He called the breakup trial by fire. Years later, we lunched in New York and he sped off on a white motorcycle.

But it was my final restaurant job, years later after I returned to Virginia with Russell, that was the most dramatic, another French restaurant in town. A boozy Frenchman, oily and charming, interviewed me, if you can call it that, he simply talked to me for one minute, asked me my experience, and said, ohkay, you can come tonight.

L'Arc de Triomphe was a combustible jar of gasoline from the start. First, there was the raging Monsieur—or Ro-bear, the French owner who came in at four o'clock in an oxford shirt as smooth and stiff as wax paper stuffed neatly in his pants circuitously around his gargantuan stomach, which contrasted sharply with his small, elegant hips. His face was smoothly shaven and handsome for the odd fifty years he had lived. Neatly slicked-back hair, and of course, French cologne emanating at every long, lunging stance he took. He was quiet, drank his café au lait, greeted you politely, ça va bien? his legs folded to display fine Italian loafers. His wife, La Madame, Mair-ee, would clack in on teetering wedges, a Gallic sprite with a cascade of wild golden locks and a beautiful face with damage, cigarette in hand. There were quiet phone calls to purveyors, the piping squeak of her bonjour to the odd bread seller or meat delivery man. All was peaceful, as the Mexican and El Salvadoran cooks and prep arrived in solid tapestry. Bachata music started up in the kitchen, and I would've just finished arranging the burgundy folded napkins at each table. My mise-en-place not quite done, I prepared the butter dishes. The smells arrived from the kitchen seductively as five o'clock rolled around, and I would change into my crisp white shirt. The door filled with customers and I began the whirlwind dance that is waiting on tables—spinning, remembering eight things at once, another ice tea, zucchini soup, medium rare, one white wine, two Merlot, do you take Visa? By now, Ro-bear had a white wine in his shaking hand, and the subtle snipes began, in hushed and snorted half-phrases of French. After eight o'clock, at the height of dinner, the tables chock-a-block full, the room a babble of glass, tinkling stainless steel, porcelain and laughter, another sweating white wine in his hand, who knew how many at this point, five, six? One would see, with alarm, that Ro-bear had indeed opened a bottle lying on the table. Now, drunken, his French phrases would not be subdued and English worked its way out in sharp barks as well, qu'estce'cestBITCH, what are you doin? and Mair-ee'd stab back as well. Finally at nine, nine-thirty, all standards of decorum were thrown in the garbage: Ro-bear had melted into a sweating, heaving rhino who tore drunkenly from the kitchen to the host table, swearing, the shirt completely deshabille and stained like an old picnic cloth. Any foul language came out haphazardly, startling tables right and left, in great baritone booms at Mair-ee, who catlike, snarled from the bar.

We waiters just stayed out of the way.

They ignored the customers.

People hurriedly left. Usually Ro-bear would leave in giant flourish, an inebriated "bitch" tossed as a farewell gift at the door, and cruise off in his Porsche. This was a nightly ritual, until an even more disturbing occurrence happened that catapulted everything into sheer catastrophe.

A tall moon-eyed nymph appeared one early morning at the door, asking for "job any?" Long of leg, black haired, she came from Bulgaria, was here only temporarily as an au pair. Ro-bear was seized with instant lust and tossed an apron at her. She, of course, knew nothing, could not even handle one table, completely eviscerated wine bottles with her corkscrew, dropped trays, leaving a trail of disgusted customers in her wake that we'd have to soothe. A total disaster, but Ro-bear oozed behind her every move. Mair-ee became even more snarling, a cornered cheetah with a wound now arrived in her place. Ro-bear did not hide his infatuation, he openly courted the Bulgarian with jewelry, perfumes, money. They sped off in his Porsche during the lunch breaks. It all culminated in the usual progression of drunkenness one night, as Ro-bear threw back bottle after bottle and tossed at Mair-ee every word he could utter. He barked and spit, and drew out a gleaming knife in the midst of the crowds. Granted, it was a dull stainless steel variety, one used for cutting the lemons in the bar. But it was dramatic and added flair. She screamed, swore, and called the police. They came instantly to the horror of the tables. There was a large flourish of argument as they settled the domestic squabble in the courtyard. He again flew off in his Porsche, the Bulgarian driving. The madame calmly counted the night's gains.

But he didn't come back. The next day the Lebanese waiter told me the Bulgarian and Ro-bear had gone to Boston. He had heard from the Frenchman who sold the cakes, who was Ro-bear's friend. No one knew what would happen. Fed up with the drama, I quit at the instant. The madame seemed non-plussed by it all. She simply stood at the bar, counting receipts. L'Arc de Triomphe is still there, a whole new staff scurrying.

That was the last restaurant I worked in.

❖ Pizza in a Dish

Layer in a glass bowl marinara sauce, cooked sausage, any choice of veggies, and lots of mozzarella. You can bake it until bubbly, although at Park Place, they used a microwave.

Chapter 11

Rio

Waiting for Dantinhas, 1984

After Ben, I met a Brazilian named Fernando and fell in love. He had some money, who knows from where, I had a few dollars scraped together, and we flew to Rio. The moment I entered the city it reeked of hot, old fruit and I remembered the Bahamas. A cluster of drummers jammed in the airport and he took my arm hurriedly and we ran through the halls as he saw his sister and they fell into each other's arms. She took us back to her apartment, and we entered to see five women clacking away on sewing machines, stitching leather. She designed shoes and belts as a business. We dined on shrimp and dende oil and we could hear, through the open windows of the apartment, a chorus of clattering dishes and forks, as all of Rio ate their lunch. After cafezinhos and pudim, exhausted, I fell asleep on the couch to the soft swish of their Portuguese.

The next day Fernando and I rented an apartment in Ipanema. Yes, it is true: Rio is the city of beauty and love, reeking of sex and delight, a city for lovers, for fun, for fantasy. It was blue-skied, blue-watered, lush green mountains, shiny brown bodies, dancing, drumbeats, candles burning in the night from Macumba sacrifices on all the beaches. Macumba is the African-based religion of Yoruba, full of voodoo-like lore and a host of gods and goddesses that need sacrifices. It is said the Macumbeiros can bring back the dead. The city hummed with magic and the rattle of drums, we drank cold beer with quail eggs, drank rum with crabs, the market was buzzing with flies, dende oil, coconuts cracked freshly open, every smoked pig part you can imagine, the rich smoky blanket of black beans. His family was down south in Porto Alegre. We would stay here. We were twenty-four and beautiful. I wore a *fio dental* (tiny brazilian bikini), his body gleamed like caramel. We made love incessantly in every possible way, we even broke the bathroom sink in this manner, and for the time we lived there, Fernando propped it up with a broomstick, holding the wet caulk in place to repair.

We fought as well. We had wild, screaming fights, throwing things. He seemed to ignite fires around him. He was always late, always having fun. The entire time we were in Brazil, for one year, he was waiting for a great job connection through his rich and influential uncle, Dantinhas (pronounced dan-cheenyas). Dantinhas lived in a modern glass high-rise in Rio in front of the sea, an elegant suite with a large porch covered in tropical plants. He was a small bald man, with a smooth, oily elegance, a fine lizard wrapped in silk and Italian finery, he warmly welcomed us with imported whisky in cut crystal glasses, we clabbered in on his parquet floors and a small woman brought us snacks and such, he smelled of ancient oils and kissed us many times—but the gleam of the cold-blooded reptile was there in the eyes, small and unblinking. Perhaps he was a gangster or dealt in illegal things, I didn't know, but I felt the trickle of cold air from somewhere. He promised Fernando a job, and with his computer skills this would come quickly, he said. You just need to wait. Dantinhas is very connected, said Fernando.

So, we waited. We lounged on the beach and ate camarones in the shell. We stuffed ourselves with feijoada, a black bean stew with pork, and caipirinhas, cascinha de siri (stuffed crab), endless cold cerveca by the beach of Buzios. We'd have grilled chicken with bananas, xuxu de camaron, a luscious shrimp stew with coconut and palm oil. We made love, fought, and ate, in no particular order. The money slowly trickled away. Someone had to work. Fernando was always calling Dantinhas from various pay phones, to no avail.

I decided to teach English. After an interminable bus ride, I interviewed at a shabby building from the sixties, square with bad geometric decorations, miles away on the outskirts of town. I would teach English and make a few cruzeiros an hour (the money at the time, it changed rapidly). It was all depressing, and the balloon of glamour that is Rio had started to deflate. In the afternoon, we went to the beach and lolled, soaking in my last days of Cariocan indolence. Up and down the beach, hawkers shouted out their wares, and they sell everything— cut coconuts, tiny bikinis, jewelry, crab, shrimp, and most of all—sandwiches. "Sanduiche natural" is the cry you hear from morning until night as they drag their little pouches around. A quick calculation in my brain, after purchasing one, made me realize they probably make much more than I would teaching

English. I talked to a few more sellers, discussed their selection. I told Fernando, and we were off "sanduiche natural" was our new mating call.

We'd have to get up early, unfortunately, for two young sloths, and go to the market. We were careful to buy whole wheat bread, as was the trend, and we doctored up our tuna and egg salad—we added curry to our tuna and avocado and herbs to our egg salad. We bought plastic wrap and I practiced my Portuguese for the new selections. We turned our little apartment into a factory, just like his sister, and hit the beach, making sure we were there just at twelve he went one way, I went the other, and I shyly started my sanduiche natural cry. Some people laughed—who was this gringa? A blond American, selling sanduiche? Because of this, so many groups would flag me down, laughing—what are you doing? Groups of Germans chortled, smiled, bought five sanduiches. English, astonished, heard my story, and bought four sanduiches. I explained they were different, special flavors, and they actually loved them. This was my first catering job. I sold out rapidly.

Fernando came running down the beach, ecstatic. You have to understand his speech—he had a very strong Portuguese accent, and he seemed to stutter a bit when excited. He'd oddly add a few extra syllables in randomly, as in "Nani, I abodee abbodah went to the abodee store." When my brother knew him for a while, he'd say, what, what what was that extra stuff you just said, that abodee aboduh business? No one knew. It was just Fernando. So he came running up up, "Nani! Abodee aboduh, I sold all my sandwich! All!"

Me, too! I said. We were off and running. People started to look for us, track us down. Our sandwiches were really good, and people started to have favorites, so we'd adjust and invent new flavors.

But we started to have issues. We'd stay out late, frittering away our new money and not wake up early, I'd yell at Fernando, get your ass in gear! It's twelve, and he'd be drinking his cafezinho blearily. Here is where our sanduiche natural enterprise hit the skids, and went bankrupt—we just wanted to have fun. He wanted to drink his coffee, drink caipirinhas all day, dance samba until four. He was Brazilian, and one thing they do well, is enjoy life. They love life, they eat life, and that's who he was. I was screaming at him in my American capitalist manner and he couldn't take it. He flung all the sandwiches out the window, and they landed—smash, right in the middle of Avenida Vieira Souto. Motherfucker, I lunged at him, we screamed and tousled like cheetahs, and ended up making love on the kitchen floor.

He called Dantinhas, again.

Our money was almost gone.

The party was over. We packed up our bags and went down south to Porto Alegre. The bus took hours and hours, stopping at a churrasco restaurant for one magic hour where we stuffed ourselves on roasted meats of every ilk, and then we arrived, weary and broke.

In Porto Alegre, a city known for gauchos (Brazilian cowboys) and maté (a hot green tea drunk out of a gourd), not much changed, except we lived with his parents. Now the phone calls to Dantinhas included his father. Always Dantinhas said, "Maybe next week."

I couldn't talk to anyone so I started going to the library on a daily basis by bus to study Portuguese. The only books they had were ancient, from the fifties, so I was learning strange archaic phrases that made everyone laugh. The other thing I did was draw fashions all day long. Fernando was convinced we could hook up with his sister in Rio and open a shop, so I worked on the designs. He waited for Dantinhas.

Finally, an interview arrived.

It was in the old section of Porto Alegre, in an ancient colonial building, and I came with him. He was met by two pale and slim bureaucrats holding clipboards. It was some sort of computer firm and of course they needed English skills. I could see Fernando from a corner in the waiting room where I sat, but not the "team." They started in Portuguese. I noticed Fernando started getting nervous, sweat had appeared on his forehead. He kept wiping it off. Then, they progressed to English, which by now, after six months back in Brazil, had severely lapsed. The sweat came in waves now, I believe he was shaking and the "abodee abodah" stutter came roaring in. It was painful. I couldn't help him, just watch him fumble, I abodee abodah a stud in Washeen-ton D.C.

The Brazilian accent always cuts off the end of words, as in study to stud. Which gave great delight to my parents, when Fernando announced to them, with pride, Ann, John, I came to this country to stud and to stud only.

It was obvious it was a flop, but I congratulated him and we came home buoyant and eager. His parents clapped his back and hugged. But I had seen defeat, and said nothing. He held on to some hope they would call, and when they didn't, slowly he accepted, and it was back to calling Dantinhas and waiting. We would spend our nights playing snooker and sharing an Atlantica beer. During the day, I would take my little bus to the library in town and study, eating lunch at the small lancheria in the library, which made a toasted ham and cheese sandwich in an old-fashioned griddle that compressed the whole thing, like a laundry iron. Fernando, however, became more and more agitated with my library venture, convinced I was meeting a man in town. Even accompanying me didn't soothe him, he would fly into jealous rages. His overbearing possessiveness started to get to me and I developed a weird social phobia, becoming nervous when talking to any man, especially in his presence. I would blush and start shaking, and it became a problem. I couldn't talk to his father or brother without panicking, blushing, stammering. I went to the drugstore to find something for my nerves, but all I could find was something called maracujina, which was a diminutive of the word maracuja, which is passion fruit. The juice of passion fruit is quite delicious and is considered to be a relaxant for children. This concentrated tincture I believe was for hyperactive children, but I would consume cups of it in order to somehow fix my social ills. Fernando became so sensitive, if I beat him at snooker, he would fly into a rage. I now wore sunglasses at all times, even at the dinner table, to the surprise of his family. I avoided talking to all men. I read books and drew. I would cook for the family, Indian food, chocolate chip cookies, turkey, anything to keep me busy. I went back to life of my childhood—cooking, drawing, reading. I started to miss the U.S., the ease of it all. My family.

I finally approached Fernando and said I was leaving. He could come "later." I bought a round-trip ticket, but secretly I hoped to stay forever and extricate myself from this odd life. The culmination came when I beat him at snooker and he punched me in the arm. I packed my bags and left.

Back home, I arrived feeling weak and alone. We went from the airport to the supermarket to pick up a few things. I was stunned. Everything was clean, wrapped in plastic. No smells of rotting fruit, no flies. No batucada drum group beating away in some corner. No guranana, no black beans in huge piles by the kilo. No hunks of smelly meat hanging.

I went to my room and all the old loneliness of my childhood came back, just me in an old farmhouse, in the midst of 350 acres, nowhere to go, nothing to do but cook, read, or draw. I would have to get a job, move to the city, but I was in some horrible underwater inertia. I lay in my room and listened to sad, plaintive music from Bahia.

After one week, I was back on a plane to Brazil. I felt shaky and confused, dizzy, still the ubiquitous sunglasses. When I entered the spotlight brilliance of Brazil, I didn't feel better, just relieved. I came back to the same pattern, Dantinhas, sleeping late, a long lazy lunch, afternoon siesta, sunglasses, going to the library, snooker at night, fighting, all over again. We had been here one year and Fernando had no job, besides our beach sandwich gig. We were tired, burned out, tired of each other. We finally packed our bags and went to the USA, where at least we knew he could work.

At Greenwood, it wasn't much better. We sat around here as well. Fernando became obsessed with Macumba spirits, that we were the victims of a bad evil eye, and he gave sacrifices to the Orishas. He went hunting from early dawn to dusk, dragging back deer. He went fishing in the trickle of a river called Goose Creek and brought back bags of tiny silver fish, which he deep-fried and served with lemon. He always blended any kind of fruit he could find, from the market or wild from a tree with sugar and froze it, and he always had a bubbling pot of black beans on the stove. Ann and John were long suffering, and actually liked him very much. He was always the life of the party, loud, dancing. Everyone noted his dark good looks. We had no car and no money. I found someone who drove into D.C. every morning at nine, and I commuted with him in order to work in a Vie de France bakery on K Street at eleven, then I had to kill time in the afternoon as well, until I waited for my ride back at six, I was saving money, and meanwhile Fernando lived in the woods, hunting, trapping, fishing. We stopped arguing and basically circumnavigated each other in the evenings. He barbecued for my parents and played soccer. He slept late and woke up to his frozen fruit batidas.

Eventually, everything so disintegrated between us, and I had saved some money, so I went to live with an old friend. Fernando stayed on the farm. After a while, I started dating other people and Fernando dated others, but he still lived on the farm. My parents said, What's going on with Fernando? Should we start calling him Uncle Fernando?

The end of Brazil and Fernando was sad, and drawn out. I miss the beans, the drums, the smell of the country. I miss the Sunday barbecues with his family, grilling all meats and beef hearts and sharing a large wooden jar of caipirinhas between us all. The way his eighty-year-old grandmother would get up and shake to samba music. Carnival in the stadium at Porto Alegre, coming back covered in glitter, a pittering beat still throbbing in your ears. The tiny lancheria at the library. The rosy evening sky over Ipanema. Sanduiche natural!

Eventually, he went back to Brazil, not to be heard from, until suddenly years later: he called my brother and wanted to have a barbecue. He had arrived from Brazil with his new wife, Verucia. He would come to John's house, feed us all Brazilian barbecue. He wanted me to come, and I did, with my husband, two children. We ate grilled meats with yucca powder and laughed all day. There is that odd feeling when you are with an old lover, the intimacy gone but still remembered by both, even as you talk of mundanity, how's your mother? Your brother? It is a tiny light, not a roaring fire, but it burns just the same and it is only for the two of you, never to be again, never to be replaced. It is like the light of the small Macumba altars set up on the beaches of Rio at night, a bottle of cachaca alongside, the wind dousing the flame to a small dot and then it bursts up and flickers in the sea air for a few minutes. It will burn all night, a small yellow flame against the deep blue of the Brazilian waters. It will not be seen in the harsh yellow light of day, as people laugh and work and walk on by, pushing sand, hawkers yelling, the drum beats. But at night, there is again, that candlelight, flickering.

❖ Feijoada

    1 pound dried black beans
    1 pound smoked ham hocks
    1 pound Brazilian linguiça (any type pork sausage will do)
    ½ pound smoked pork or beef ribs
    ½-pound piece lean Canadian bacon or Brazilian *carne seca*
    1 large onion, coarsely chopped
    3 garlic cloves, finely chopped or crushed
    4 tablespoons olive or vegetable oil
    3 to 4 strips smoked bacon (optional)
    1 small pork tenderloin, cubed
    1 tablespoon white vinegar

Salt and black pepper to taste
1 teaspoon cayenne pepper
Hot sauce (optional)

Soak beans overnight in large container. In large pot, cook beans for 4 to 5 hours over low heat. Meanwhile, place ham hocks, sausage, ribs, and Canadian bacon in deep pan with plenty of water and bring to boil. Change water and bring to a new boil, repeating the procedure at least three times to tenderize cured meats and remove excess fat. In large frying pan, sauté onion and garlic using 2 tablespoons of either olive or vegetable oil (smoked bacon strips optional) for 2 or 3 minutes. Toss in cubed pork. Sauté for additional 2 to 3 minutes.

Mash 5 to 10 tablespoons of beans, and return to the large pot of beans. The resulting paste will thicken sauce. Add the remaining 2 tablespoons of the olive oil, vinegar, salt, black pepper, and cayenne. Stir, heat over medium fire for 2 to 3 minutes, then transfer to contents of frying pan. (You may use two frying pans, if necessary.) Let simmer for 10 to 15 minutes. Add contents of frying pan(s) to the beans and let simmer at medium heat for 1 to 2 hours.

Serve the feijoada over rice, with additional red-hot sauce if desired, sliced oranges, and farofa.

❖ Xuxu de Galinha

One 3- to 4-pound chicken, cut into serving pieces
Juice of 2 lemons
Salt and black pepper
¼ pound dried smoked shrimp, peeled
1 large onion, quartered
2 ripe medium tomatoes, peeled, seeded, and coarsely
    chopped
2 tablespoons olive oil
1 garlic clove, minced

1 pound jumbo shrimp, peeled
4 preserved malagueta peppers, or to taste
2 tablespoons ground roasted cashew nuts
1 tablespoon ground roasted peanuts
½ tablespoon minced fresh ginger
3 tablespoons dendê oil (substitute made from 1 cup vegetable oil and 3 tablespoons annatto seeds that have been soaked for 12 hours)

Marinate the chicken in the lemon juice and salt and pepper to taste for half an hour; then drain and set aside. Grind dried shrimp in food processor with onion and tomatoes into thick paste. In large saucepan, heat oil over medium heat. Add garlic and cook, stirring, until browned. Add onion-tomato-shrimp paste and drained chicken pieces. Brown chicken pieces all over, then add ¼ cup water bit by bit, cover pot, reduce heat to low, and cook for 35 to 40 minutes, until chicken is almost cooked. Be sure that mixture does not boil and stir occasionally so that chicken pieces do not stick to pan. Add jumbo shrimp, malagueta peppers, and nuts. Check seasonings. Add ginger and ½ cup water and finish cooking by bringing mixture to boil. When ready to serve, drizzle dendê over the xu-xu and cook for a few more minutes. Serve hot with white rice and farofa.

Chapter 12

Mexico

Chasing Butterflies and Fears, 1997

Years later, I'm married with kids, it was springtime and we decided to pack the kids up and go to Mexico to see the migration of the monarch butterflies, something I had heard was magical. After a tortuous four-bus journey through the state of Michoacan, we emerged into Angangueo, a town with only one hotel. It was late at night, we didn't have reservations, and we had two small children. Someone in an old battered truck knew a place, he drove us up the hill and I waited for a terrible twenty minutes as my husband went inside a shack to discuss lodging. At this point, I thought he was killed, I was burned out, exhausted, desperate for comfort and shelter. My ex-husband and I never could travel together, and perhaps here was where the difference became sharp and unavoidable. We were wired differently in the most clashing way—I had lived an insecure childhood and need safety, and comfort—he lived a solid, suburban upbringing and craved danger. This train-wrecked quite beautifully on this night as I lost it in the parking lot with two Mexican men in an old truck as I feared for my life, with my two niños. I sobbed, tired and burned out. I didn't want to see any fucking butterflies. At this point, traveling with chickens and weird men in the bus who whispered strange and horrible things in my ear (be careful in the villages . . . they will take your children . . . kill you and your husband . . . now I realize he was crazy or evil) and the smell of shit everywhere, at two in the morning, I craved the safest, most boring American sterility—a Holiday Inn, a crisp-sheeted bed, cleanliness. I was spent.

He came out, prompted by the men. What's wrong, he asked with such naiveté to who I was as a person (this is no doubt where I realized he was not my hero, and yes, ultimately, all women do want a hero). He tried to talk me into staying in the ominous mountain shack with these feral men who resembled Hollywood's worst depiction of border drug runners who belonged to a gang called El Fuerte Macho. I begged for anything, anywhere. Finally, one of them said: I know a place, in his grumbling Spanish. It was a place in the town, certainly not perfect, not The Four Seasons, a simple lodging house, which I joyfully entered as if Shangri-La's doors had opened, and where, on a pea-green polyester blanket I sobbed for all my terror, for the horrible fantasy I had imagined, slaughtered in the mountains by a rambling bunch of roadsters, my children sold as slaves.

In the soft early morning mist, the men came back to get us and drive us up the mountain to the oyamel forest where the winged insects lived. It was all a fairy tale by now, and the ferocious men of last night had become gentle, worn Mexican men with shabby clothes in the light of day, carefully assisting my small son into the truck, who were making a buck as only they knew how in the height of the butterfly season. I was drained and self-admonished, and yet I knew myself clearer now. I could not survive this type of insecurity one more time, having lived through it my whole life. I needed to feel protected. Another thread between me and Russell fell away. No wonder I had a phobia driving on highways, I felt out of control and afraid of where I was going. I somberly took all this in as we climbed raggedly, roughly over the biggest boulder-clad mountain. I wondered how anyone had ever found these butterflies, in this faraway forest. The truck tossed and buckled as if it might flip at any moment.

We emerged into a green valley so lovely, where fires smoldered in small lean-tos, and blue corn grew in rows. We got out, because we would be walking from now on, but not before I entered a small shack of corrugated tin, with my kids, and smelled the wildly satisfying smell of long-simmered beans over a fire. It was a small café of sorts, the simplest in the world, with hardly a selection, but shattered and feeling as battered as the old trucks, my friend, food, would be my comfort. And I did enjoy one of the best meals I have ever tasted: the smokiest beans ladled onto a chipped enamel plate, sprinkled with a local cotija goat cheese, and homemade, fire-toasted blue corn tortillas. I was insanely grateful, cowered with gratefulness at the explosion of taste and the translucently blue sky that suddenly popped out from the early morning mist. A small boy named Mario became our guide, he joyfully teased and chased our kids up the long walk, to the oyamel forest.

And the butterflies? A velvet world of pattering, as if rain is falling but it is not. A breathy wind of wings all around, an orange satin covering on every ledge, branch, walk, a beating of staccato velveteen wings. Magical, yes, but frightening, how delicacy in numbers is ferocious and loud.

After the butterflies we ended up in San Miguel, a colonial town nestled in the mountains, arid and dusty, a lovely green square with boiled corn and balloons, young lovers perched under the trees and bathed in a soft, sweet peacefulness. It is a town of crowing roosters, cobbled streets, donkeys, and tamales sold from a tiny Indian woman's colorful shoulderbag, as well as clusters of American pale octogenarians in ponchos. You can eat sushi (though who would??) if you care to, or dine in a centuries-old chapel, aglow with hundreds of santos candles and dine on huitlacoche crêpes. On our first trip there, we found a night party on the top mountain, with the whole town invited to watch an eclipse. People were European, Russian, Mexican, American, from all corners of the world, milling about in the dark, grasping candles. Children scurried in eager groups. Ladies milled hawking black bean tamales to warm us in the cool mountainous air and a small crowlike man sold shots of tequila in tiny red earthenware glasses. At one quick moment, the moon disappeared and there were murmurs and gasps in all languages, ululating in the cold black air. It was quite lovely, and I vowed to come back.

And so I did, to write all my books, from 2000 on. I stayed in a rented house on many occasions with other writers, with a cook named Juana. We would write all day, take a break for lunch, then sally forth again, breaking in the evening to chat and socialize, go outside to the restaurants of town. Juana seemed quiet and distant, until one day I happened to stroll out in the courtyard where she was serving the gardener a snack. I guess she noticed my large fountain of drool, because she quickly offered me a small snack as well, which was fantastic— baby Swiss chard she had just picked, sautéed with chiles, onions, and garlic, all snuggled in a fresh tortilla with a sprinkling of queso fresco. After that, we strangely became buddies. She would make us platters of chilequiles and bowls of tortilla soup for our lunch breaks, and a big crock of chunky guacamole and freshly fried chips for our evenings when we would break from our writing, swigging bad wine we'd purchased in town.

She told me about the best markets in town, and I would leave my computer and forage—coming back with neon Mexican woven plastic sacks full of giant papayas, tiny sweet bananas, jícama, avocados. I'd spend hours in the market, mainly eating, skipping writing.

I am a street food aficionado, I risk all. I adore the Mexican shrimp "coctel," served in a liquidy sauce in a large margarita glass with saltines. Delicious fruit "botanas" blended with papaya and mango. Quesadillas with spicy mushrooms, which are actually, to our terms, more like deep-fried turnovers. And my favorite, the huarache, a crisp corn tortilla that resembles the famous sandal, with papas and nopales, drizzled with green salsa. Street tacos are good, too, with roasted meats and a sprinkle of cilantro and onion. But even I had to forgo the carne crua tostada I once mistakenly ordered in San Miguel, and when I saw the raw meat, I had to throw away.

After my divorce, I came back to Mexico with a friend named Michael. We were not romantically involved, but we shared an intense and emotional friendship, almost like siblings. We would be working on a musical together, a thing I had been casually playing with called "Barry, Light of Lights." We somehow found a small house in San Miguel with a portable keyboard, and a sweet round-faced cook who would make us lunch. Michael had never been there, and like anyone who comes here, was instantly and completely charmed. We awoke early and went to our separate offices (mine was the kitchen), I writing the story, he writing the music.

We had conflicts, he felt I was making the characters too intense, I felt he simplified them too much. I wanted to write a song or two, he wanted to do all the songs. We had one real argument that almost broke out in tears. We retreated and cooled down, but I knew working with someone wouldn't work for me. We also, personally, had too much cryptic baggage between us. We became friends in an acting class during the last days of my divorce. Even though he seemed to prefer men, there was unresolved sexual tension between us we both acknowledged, but never acted upon. Our tension grew and grew in the house, and I took to waking up early and watching the DVD collection in the house. I saw *Saving Private Ryan*, and my emotions felt raw and exposed. He felt the house was haunted and was having nightmares. He begged me to leave early and go to Mexico City. We left.

He wanted to go to a gay bar. I think the odd tension between us was unsettling on both sides, he sought something more familiar. We stayed in a hotel recommended by a taxi driver but it was cheesy and turned out to be a hotel of prostitutes. We were getting more and more depressed. We saw three men on the street and we asked them if they knew a good gay bar. It turned out they were celebrating one of their midst's birthday, they brought us along. It was a fun place, called The Living Room, created out of a large residential house. I danced and danced and Michael had found a beautiful young man. He wanted me to go home by myself. Here is where the tension exploded. We yelled and screamed as the people stared. I didn't care, I was burned out and fearful, he felt scared and cornered. We sobbed, and finally made up. We went back to the whore hotel and collapsed.

The young man came to say goodbye in the airport. He was dark, with Indian features, and stayed by us as we ate chilequiles in a cafeteria, polite and sweet. We left Mexico. I haven't been back since.

❖ **Chilequiles with Chicken and Tomatillo Salsa**

½ pound manchego cheese
½ pound mozzarella cheese
4 round corn tortillas
4 boneless, skinless chicken breasts
Pinch of salt
1 onion, quartered
2 garlic cloves
Vegetable oil for frying
Sour cream diluted with small amount of water
Tomatillo salsa (see below)

Shred the cheeses. Cut the tortillas into strips, but not too wide.

Put chicken in a large saucepan or skillet with a little water, the salt, onion, and garlic. Cover and slowly cook over medium heat until chicken is cooked through and tender. Put chicken on a plate and let cool for a while until you can shred in very small pieces with your hands or a fork.

Deep-fry the corn tortillas in a skillet with ¼-inch vegetable oil. When they are crisp, remove and drain on paper towels to remove excess oil.

Preheat oven to 350°F.

Assemble the chilaquiles like a lasagna. Using a big lasagna pan, layer as follows: layer of tortillas; layer of chicken in sauce; add dollops of salsa; a few dots of diluted sour cream; cheese.

Repeat for next layers and finish with cheese and some sour cream.

Bake for about 45 minutes, until golden and bubbly.

◈ Tomatillo Salsa

1½ pounds fresh tomatillos or three 11-ounce cans
   tomatillos
5 fresh serrano chiles
3 garlic cloves (not peeled)
½ cup chopped fresh cilantro
1 large onion, coarsely chopped
2 teaspoons coarse salt (Kosher or sea salt)

Preheat broiler.

If using fresh tomatillos, remove husks and rinse under warm running water to remove stickiness. If using canned tomatillos, drain and measure out 2 cups. Broil chiles, garlic, and fresh tomatillos (do not broil canned tomatillos) on rack of broiler pan 1 to 2 inches from heat, turning once, until tomatillos are softened and slightly charred, about 7 minutes.

Peel garlic and pull off tops of chiles. Purée all ingredients in a blender.

❖ Huaraches with Papas y Chiles

2 cups dehydrated masa flour (corn tortilla flour)
1 teaspoon baking powder
¼ teaspoon salt plus more as needed
1¾ cups chicken broth
2 cups refried beans

Topping
½ cup diced cooked potato
½ cup peeled, sliced green fresh poblano chiles
2 cups shredded cabbage
½ cup tomato or green tomatillo salsa
¼ cup crumbled cotija or feta cheese
¼ cup sour cream
Black pepper

In a large bowl, mix together masa flour, baking powder, ¼ teaspoon salt, and broth until dough holds together well, adding a little water if needed.

Divide dough into four equal portions. Shape each portion into 6-inch-long log on sheet of waxed paper. Pat each log into ⅛-inch-thick oval, about 4 by 8 inches. (If shaped ahead, stack between sheets of waxed paper, wrap airtight, and refrigerate for up to 2 hours.)

Place griddle or two 10- to 12-inch frying pans over medium-high heat. When griddle is hot, flip an oval of masa dough onto it and peel off any waxed paper. Cook until bottom of huarache is light brown, about 3 minutes. Use wide spatula to turn huaraches over.

Spread about one-quarter of the beans over each huarache. Cook until huarache bottoms are lightly browned, 2 to 3 minutes. With a wide spatula, transfer to plates.

Top huaraches equally with diced cooked potato, chiles, shredded cabbage, salsa, cheese, sour cream, and salt and pepper to taste.

❖ Chicken Tortilla Soup

Five 6-inch stale corn tortillas
¼ cup corn or other vegetable oil
1 small onion, chopped
2 garlic cloves, finely chopped
3 dried medium guajillo chile
4 cups chicken broth
One 14.5-ounce can diced tomatoes, not drained
½ teaspoon coarse salt (kosher or sea salt)
1½ cups shredded cooked chicken
1 ripe medium avocado
½ cup shredded Monterey Jack cheese or other mild melting
    cheese
Chile crumbles (see below)
Chopped fresh cilantro
1 lime, cut into wedges

Cut tortillas in half; cut halves into ¼-inch strips. In 3-quart saucepan, heat half of the oil over medium-high heat. Fry strips in oil, working with one-third of strips at a time, until light brown and crisp. Remove from pan; drain on paper towels. Set aside.

Heat remaining oil in saucepan over medium-high heat. Add onion and cook for 2 minutes, stirring frequently. Add garlic and chiles; cook for 2 to 3 minutes, stirring frequently, until vegetables are crisp-tender. Stir in broth, tomatoes, and salt. Heat to boiling. Reduce heat; cover and simmer for 15 minutes. Add chicken; heat through.

To serve, pit and peel avocado and cut into 1-inch slices. Divide half of tortilla strips among four individual serving bowls; ladle soup into bowls. Top with avocado, cheese, and chile crumbles, and garnish with remaining tortilla strips and cilantro. Serve with lime wedges.

❧ Chile Crumbles

Guajillo chiles

Bake chiles on baking sheet lined with foil at 400°F for 20 minutes. Let dry until cool, then crumble and remove seeds and stems.

Chapter 13

Japan

A Tour of Essential Loneliness, 2000

When I was a child, getting on an airplane was fun, usually it was a family trip to the Bahamas. Years later, I am terrified. I have learned, however, on a free press trip to Japan in order to research a food trip for Russell's travel business that fear of flying is greatly reduced by flying on business class on someone's else's bill. Could be also be the addition of half a Xanax, or the constant fluttering attention of the flight attendants, or perhaps it's just the cardigan they pass around at the beginning, fashioned of maroon acrylic, yet somehow comforting all the same.

Arrival: I am vexed to find that it takes two hours from the Narita airport to my hotel in central Tokyo. In my completely vegetal state, I find myself musing on how interesting that the bus driver pauses at a red light and lets it change twice without moving. I'm also wondering what exactly made him decide to go for an unfashionable perm. He is a small, delicate man with a giant artificial mushroom of hair looming from his fragile skull. I know if I fall asleep, I will undoubtedly miss my hotel stop and yet I haven't slept in twenty-four hours. I'm in blur with the constant changing of neighborhoods, the clutter of Tokyo, and the bouncing perm. No sooner did I arrive at The Four Seasons, I am fast asleep only to stand just a few hours later groggily in the lobby at four A.M. awaiting a taxi to go down to the seafood wholesale market at Tsukiji. This has always been a dream of mine, and apparently this is a big tourist attraction. Mainly, I just want sushi. All the other Americans on this trip balk at sushi at 4:30 A.M., but I am ravenous to try. All along the edge of the market there are makeshift sushi bars, hung with shabby curtains. I hijack my guide, a young woman with lanky curls, and push aside the curtains to one and within a few minutes, the chef slices up his favorite selection, including a type of suzuki (whitefish) only found in Tokyo. The miso soup is floating with hunks of hamachi on the bone. The whole experience is surreal. The uni was so fresh, each piece bumpy and ochre like a cat's tongue. I almost passed out when he dished up such superb toro, a pale pink oozing with oil. Outside the frail curtain, fishmongers inspected the tuna with flashlights. Apparently, you can easily spot the oil content this way, and good tuna is all about oil content. I collapse after that gastronomic adventure. Japanese food just astounds me. Even breakfast in the hotel is euphoria, rice and fish and pickles.

One thing on my agenda was to interview some really famous Japanese sushi chef because I was trying to write a novel about one. That doesn't seem to be a problem with the Coordinators, so I am escorted to the posh and fashionable Park Hyatt, a gleaming fifty-two-floored column of sleek onyx and glass. Everyone resembles hip street urchins in perfectly ragged clothing and shaggy anime haircuts and I begin to feel like a marshmallow. You may remember the Park Hyatt from the movie *Lost in Translation*. Suddenly, it's time to meet the master sushi chef. I want to drill him about the ten years of apprenticing in the sushi field. I want to know why women are forbidden in this field (later I learn that their hands are too warm). I want to know when he cut his first slice of toro, and where he grew up, so I further formulate the character for my novel I am writing—Mr. Ito. A few minutes later I am introduced to—Brett Patterson. Obviously not Japanese, and frankly, it almost seems like a name straight from *The Young and the Restless,* and he is, it turns out, a New Zealander, who, to his credit offers me champagne and makes a lot of jokes with his cute accent. So I forget about the formidable chef I was hoping for and just titter and drink champagne. He tells me ate snapper sperm the other day and it was good. He says he was a bit concerned about it, at first. I told him, this is a universal concern. At this point, slightly drunk, we muse about how one exactly gets snapper sperm. I decide it's time I find my group and eat dinner. I proceed down to the forty-third floor and have bamboo shoots dug up in Kyoto that morning at the best restaurant in the world, Kozue. No snapper sperm, though. Fresh out. Brett Patterson refused to comment.

The next day we are given a tour guide and we are never free again. First, we have an informational meeting. Some verbatim quotes of useful tourist information in Japan provided by the guide who calls himself Mr. Smiley:

"Please don't be late to appointment because if you are late you will break face and I will break face."

"You can drink water here, if you drink water in Bangkok you get express train and go down very fast."

"Our street signs do not say walk, you have to wait for signal, so if you get run over please choose a Rolls-Royce and if happen you must crawl to sidewalk to die."

We all dutifully write these down. Then Mr. Smiley takes us to the Asakusa temple. When we are there, he pulls out a broken-off TV antenna to which he has attached a red bandanna and we follow him and yes, we look like ridiculous fools but we are powerless, controlled by his constant pointing and gesturing with the broken antenna. It occurs to me that if indeed Mr. Smiley is a professional in this industry, he could invest in a high-tech pointing device, maybe something with infrared or a tracking device. This is Japan, after all. But that musing is quickly whisked away by the interruptive swishing of the antenna. He seems to read minds and know that for one second I was not thinking of feudal Japan, but his ridiculous equipment. If we stray for one second to the many shops lining the temple walk, selling useful things like tiny kimono-clad doll key rings and such, he pulls out this little wooden soldier toy, of the type Swiss children in the 1800s received in their embroidered Christmas stockings, and it goes, loudly, clock-clock-clock and we all scurry back, bad little tourists that we are. So I never got a tiny kimono-clad doll key ring because of Mr. Smiley, and that is why, instead, I bring back gifts of packaged dried squid bought from the Narita airport.

We have dinner with Mr. Smiley in a Japanese pub where we dine on grilled ox with miso. Mr. Smiley tells us he is married and has two terriers, Stephen and Ken. Turns out, Stephen was the name of his boss for many years (one envisions the odd venting possibilities that affords—Bad Stephen! Bad! Bad).

Mr. Smiley has a sad tale of how he was "let go" from his position as a tour leader for that company, and now must fare alone in the world, gathering the occasional freelance positions, and truth to tell, Mr. Smiley seems to know everything, you can ask him about the wood in the bathroom wall of the restaurant and he will tell you it was hewn in the Edo period by a young craftsman named Tekko Watanabe, boated down the Shimanto river, stationed in Kyoto for two years, and then brought by express train to Tokyo last year, so, after a few sakes, Mr. Smiley is a hero and it just turns out walking around today he mentioned it was his birthday, so someone snuck around and got him a green tea cake and the restaurant plays this Happy Birthday tape (which, as soon as the cake is cut, they turn off abruptly, leaving our stringy voices hanging in off-key).

Then I saw Mr. Smiley naked. I mean we went to this spa in the mountains of Kanazawa, all the way on the western coast of Japan (incidentally it is in its forty-sixth generation of ownership) and we all had to wear thin blue cotton yukata robes all the time and I think Mr. Smiley was naked underneath. This place was kind of a fun park for adults, hot bubbling pools to lounge in with huge penis sculptures, karaoke rooms (my friend and I entered one whereupon a cluster of drunken Japanese guys in those robes yelled American! American! Come in! Come in!) and it even has a paint-your-own-pottery place, where one night we found Mr. Smiley painting a teacup with a little picture of Stephen and Ken. They can be a real pain, he said, because he has to wash their paws every time they come in from outside.

Naked (under his robe), Mr. Smiley tells us how he got married, how he selected his wife (she seemed okay from picture and I meet her, not too bad, then I pay her family). I was unaware that this sort of thing happened in Japan, though I don't probe further. He shows us a picture of an attractive women in a sweatsuit, with Stephen and Ken. I ask him, do you have any children? No, just Stephen and Ken, he says.

Other interesting things about Mr. Smiley: he collects phone cards. He repeatedly asked us if we had any used phone cards for his collection. One would think one time would sufficiently answer this question, but, no, Mr. Smiley continued to ask on a daily basis and I really started to wonder for Stephen, Ken, and the purchased wife. And he watches the antiques channel in his spare time. He says he came from a very rich family but they lost everything during wartime. He calls himself Mr. Smiley because he says his name is too unpronounceable. He gave us a printout of our itinerary every day that said, no holy socks, and despite his fascist antenna, truth to tell, he is very amazing man, a hard worker, a lover of dogs.

Somehow, I manage to convince Mr. Smiley that I need a few hours off from the relentless touring. I need to visit the market. I am, after all, researching a food tour in Japan, but on a daily basis I am traipsing through every palace and temple Japan has to offer. After much struggle, he agrees, but only with a guide. A guide! It seems one is forbidden to venture forth unaccompanied. I argue more, and finally I am free. I feel like a teenager driving for the first time. I wander the town market of Kanazawa, giddy and euphoric. The seafood markets are the best, bustling with indescribable heaps of ocean matter, dozens of clams and oysters I've never seen, periwinkles, sea urchins. Piles of beautiful bright orange crabs the size of baseball mitts. I wander through neighborhoods, smelling the air, which always has the sweetish resiny flavor of boiling sake. I smell this smell all over Japan, and this, along with the tang of Bulgari green tea perfume, which is what every soap and shampoo is perfumed with at the Tokyo Four Seasons, becomes the scent of Japan to me forever.

I linger at a karaoke booth in the seafood market, wanting to venture inside. They are only the size of a McDonald's restroom. I'd really like to sing "I Did It My Way," in a Japanese accent. It seems to be the Japanese salaryman's national anthem, sung drunkenly in about every karaoke spot in the country. I am amazed at how earnest everyone is. They try so hard to do a good job, from Mr. Smiley to this driven little taxi driver I had in Kyoto days before. We gave him directions to a couple's house who lived on the outskirts of the national park, in a large modern Western-style house. Not having street numbers, it was virtually impossible to find. The poor man, decked in immaculate white gloves and a shiny patent leather cap, drove us around and then stopped every ten minutes to ask directions at various houses.

I want to enter the karaoke stall, but it seems there is someone inside. I heard teenagers have sex in these, so I leave. I'll have plenty more opportunities to sing in Japan.

I tried to break away from the tour another time in Kyoto, but Mr. Smiley insisted that I be accompanied by the respectable president of the ladies' society. In order to meet this woman, first we had to attend a tea ceremony, which, though very beautiful, lasted for two hours without much happening, and afterward we were given a small ball of green skin, called a rice cake. I know all about my insolent American ways, feverish people without attention spans, brought up on MTV and constant ads and information overload, etc. etc., but this was really remarkably tedious. There seems to be a certain pleasure, a masochistic delight, in the pure tedium of watching water boiling and then whisked for hours. And then, I needed to meet this nice lady for touring of the food markets of Kyoto. I really longed to break free. First of all, I wanted to sample every piece of street food I saw, but I felt hindered by the society lady, in her lovely kimono, so I couldn't. I was caught in a quandary in Japan—wanting to break free and do my own thing, yet being part and parcel of an incredibly generous press trip that allowed me access into parts of the culture I never would've seen. It mirrors, in some part, the dilemma of my whole life, wanting to be part of some meaningful community or relationship, and in the end, not able to handle the suffocation that comes with this, breaking free and seeking freedom. But oh the food of Japan. Who can even begin to compare to the way the Japanese respect seafood, the unfailingly vibrant regard for quality and taste that they have cultivated? On my trip, none of the journalists seemed to get it—invariably, at a banquet somone would push their plate along to me with a loud Yuck, and I would have a surplus of the rarest whale liver in Japan, or a pile of translucent raw squid, and no one to share the amazing moment.

The Japanese, so proper seeming, with their intricate manners and respect, just love to do a complete flip around, and become impertinent and ribald. I worked in a sushi bar for a few years in Washington, D.C., after returning from Brazil, before my marriage. Way before I was writing, but the experience obviously colored my first novel, *Crawling at Night*. The various dirty jokes with anatomically similar sushi products were infinite. How many times had they all snickered as they waved around a flailing giant clam? Akagai, a red clam, apparently was the female equivalent, and they often asked my friend Leslie and I as we started our shift, Akagai gengki? in other words, is your vagina okay? and we'd reply dutifully, yes, thank you. Leslie really knew how to add a fillip of naughtiness to her answers for the staff, she dated one of them, after all, she'd say, verrrrry gengki, thank you, to their delight.

If you had a boyfriend, then a typical polite repartee would start like thus:

Konnichiwa, Nani-chan. Gengki?

Hai, gengki des, thank you.

How Chris?

Very well, thanks.

Good technician? followed by a huge burst of laughter from staff. Apparently, this was a hoot. Anyway, there was something charming in the question, naive and simple. As if technology was the answer to romance.

It was a man named Yukio who ran the restaurant, sleek and fast, perpetually dressed in black. I've known him for twenty years and he hasn't aged. He says funny things. I asked about the words to a Japanese song once, he replied, oh, uh, jealousy, I gotta do it. He told me once Jennifer Lopez had come into the restaurant and I asked if she was pretty. Butt okay, but face like a monkey, he said astutely. Or, when he had a restaurant in Barcelona for a year, I asked him how that experience was. Spanish people, face never move. Always sad. Simple, to the point, was his style.

It was the staff meals in the shop that were the best times, full of the ribald jokes and Japanese home cooking. Tempura soba was a favorite, buckwheat noodles with fish broth and crunchy fried tempura shrimp on top, or yakisoba, fried noodles served around temples. Occasionally, I'd make these meals, trying to imitate Japanese cooking. Yukio taught me how to add ice cubes to tempura batter for perfect crispiness or how to use a toothpick during cooking to keep the shrimp perfectly straight (Japanese apparently don't like curled shrimp). I learned how to cut vegetables properly, which took the most time and practice, especially carrots. Even broccoli had to have a honed point at the end. The knives were steel works of art, and they spent many hours sharpening them on water-covered stones. They cared for you as an employee in a parental way, feeding you, advising you, even paying your bills when business was slow. One day the wiry, bad-breathed cook left in a huff and I, the employee meal doyenne, was chosen to fill in. Not an easy task, suddenly being asked to fry tempura and prepare sukiyaki in large amounts. Copious burned piles of dough were thrown away. My broths seemed either too salty or watery. Thankfully, I was replaced after a month.

Yukio ran as if on restless overdrive, as if perpetually tripping over his toes. He wouldn't eat for hours, then collapsed at the counter hunkered over a steaming bowl of rice, green tea, and salmon skin, a Japanese housewife's favorite. Leftover rice, salmon, green tea, and lots of wasabi and shredded nori.

Yukio started running faster and faster. My friend Leslie dated him briefly but that was over quickly, he left her promptly for someone else. He went through women as if changing clothes, unthinkingly. He had been married four times. Sleek Iranian drug dealers dressed in Hugo Boss and gold and beautiful Korean women started hanging around. Yukio opened a nightclub downtown.

One day, however, he left the shop and walked down to a bookstore down the street that had opened its wares on tables out front. In a strange frenzy, his wiry black-swathed body whirled out of control and Yukio began knocking all the books to the floor. People from the restaurant were called and they held him down. An ambulance and police came, and they took Yukio away. After a rest, he came back and no one talked about the incident. The Iranians stopped coming. Yukio slowed down, ate tempura soba, shuffled instead of tripping.

Last time I was there, he had opened a new wing, all in white with shark tanks. There was a party going on and a naked woman lay coolly on a long, marble table with sashimi on her stomach, illuminated by the metallic flash of cameras and cell phones, and I saw Yukio there, in black as always, Nani-chan, gengki? Akagai gengki?

❖ Ochazuke

This is perfect leftover food, soothing and sharp.

¾ cup leftover rice (if it's cold, heat up a bit in the microwave)
Leftover salmon bits, crumbled
Salt, to taste
Hot, plain green tea
Wasabi paste
Shredded nori

Put the rice in a bowl. Top with salmon and add a bit of salt to taste. Pour hot green tea over rice. Add wasabi to taste and shredded nori last.

❖ Yakisoba

6 ounces pre-steamed yakisoba noodles
Vegetable oil

¼ pound pork, thinly sliced
½ carrot, peeled and cut into small rectangles
¼ onion, thinly sliced
1 green bell pepper, cut into small rectangles
2 cabbage leaves, cut into bite-size pieces
4 to 6 tablespoons yakisoba sauce or yakisoba seasoning
    powder (available in yakisoba kits)
Ao-nori (powdered green seaweed)
Beni-shoga (pickled red ginger)

Loosen yakisoba noodles and set aside. Heat a little oil in a wok or frying pan and fry pork.

Add carrot, onion, and green pepper to wok and stir-fry. Add cabbage and stir-fry. Add noodles. Pour ¼ cup water over noodles and cover wok. Turn heat to low and steam for a few minutes. Remove lid and add yakisoba sauce or seasoning powder. (Adjust amount of sauce according to your taste.) Add noodles and stir-fry. Serve yakisoba on plates. Sprinkle with ao-nori, and garnish with beni-shoga.

Chapter 14

Kerala

A Lost Friend, 1997

When I lived in Brooklyn, I befriended Stella, the nanny of an Indian doctor couple. She had a wheedly voice, shrill and incoherent. She was a Jehovah's Witness. She occasionally would rattle on about certain religious angles, but when I showed little response, and reacted more to her food, she became my Indian food mentor.

It's funny how the brain works. When we wonder where someone is from, and they respond, I am from India, South India, Kerala, there are so many levels of interpretation. Any connection, fabled or real, anecdotal, hearsay or fact, any sensual snippet, even any piece of dialogue are all woven instantly into a perception quilt of the subject, in this case: Kerala.

I have not been to India. I have two Indian members of my family, an uncle, a Sikh, and I barely remember him, because he lives in San Antonio married to my aunt but I remember their wedding dimly at an early age, all of us crowding around a buffet table in someone's house eating lunch, his dark flat face below a large turban, and the way he said my aunt Jenny's name, Jaynie, Jaynie, and this memory illogically came up again once when I studied Jainism in a world religion class in high school, a branch of Hinduism so pacifist they wear veils to prevent inadvertently breathing in insects. And, my half sister married an art student from from New Delhi named Chopi, and she even lived there for years. She had a striking wedding, swathed in a red sari and bestooned by henna.

But I have fiddled with Indian food for years. I adore Indian food, the rich blanket of warm spices, the deep mustard colors, the incensous smell, the overall earthiness, the smoke. I've tried to make everything, grinding spices, popping seeds, all on my own until Stella came on the scene. I knew nothing of South India, I was self-trained in the traditional northern route of rogan josh and garam masala, the same curries and flavors in every Indian restaurant in town. So when I met Stella, and she said "Kerala," I was flooded with four million incompatible thoughts and memories: Jaynie, Jaynie, the turban, my brother-in-law Chopi, my sister's white face in the red sari, Carol, my mother's friend when I was young, *Streetcar Named Desire* (Stella!), my cooking attempts, oh, it went on, all lasting a millisecond, leaving an impression no doubt subjective and unreasonable and nothing to do with the truth.

She became my best and only friend for a time. We had little in common, aside from an interest in cooking. Her ward, Tejas, a shiny-eyed boy like a wiry elf and my son Ivan played together. We would see each other formally at all the preschool happenings, the drops and pickups, and our children had bonded. Inadvertently, one day I dropped off Ivan when she had been steaming idlis. What are those, I nosily asked. This is idli, she said, scooping a hot, white bun dripping with sambal sauce in my waiting mouth. Fluffy and bland, the perfect counterpoint to the curry-leaf flavored sauce, I was instantly smitten. I hadn't had these flavors before, these odd musky curry leaves. And that's how it began. On a daily basis, I would come by and a new specialty would be served in the vegetarian Brahman household, seared eggplant stew, curried cauliflower, dosai, which are paper-thin crêpes also for sambal. I was nursing a child, starving and insatiable, but Stella was also so kind and funny with her funny voice and sharp personality.

We became closer, and she started to unfold flashes and bits of her life. Apparently, Stella had been married once. It was a sore subject I broached once, where she snorted (she often snorted) and made it clear marriage would never happen again. She told me he was not good. She hinted at beatings. Worse, she had a child she somehow lost in the transaction, and she told me a few glowing details about this daughter, but then she grew silent and the air-conditioning unit buzzed loudly in the background. I guess I was probing too much, so I left that subject. But later, after she felt comfortable again she would talk of her days in Kerala with the unkind man and her daughter. I then realized she had not lost the daughter per se, but had sacrificed being with her in order to come here and earn money, to send for her education in beauty school. When I left her house, she would give me samples of some of her cooking, a small tiffin put into my hands. Maybe because I was nursing she felt a need to feed me. It was very kind, not only because her food was amazing, enchanting, but I felt cared for.

She taught me how to make those idlis, and I even bought an idli metal steamer tray with her in a field trip to Jackson

Heights that we took together, combing the stores for bags of spices and clusters of greens. We had dosais, and tea. We stopped for sweets, gluey and delicious.

With idlis, one needs sambar, a liquidy dip made of curry leaves and spices one dips the bland idlis in for flavor. She taught me biryani, all types of vegetable curries, fish curry in coconut milk and the ubiquitous curry leaf, and a wonderful cauliflower cooked in mustard seeds, cilantro, and fresh coconut. I often spent time at their small Brooklyn townhouse, always aromatic, though almost barren in furniture and decor, as if spice silently filled in the rafters with its decorative olfactory presence. I grew comfortable with the young doctor couple as well, Padmini and Ganesh. They invited me to their parties, a large crowd of Indian medical types and scientists, politely sitting, awaiting the food, which they served in large metal tins, indecorously. I was a caterer at the time, used to the artful baby eggplant, the basil sprig, the copper chaffer. None of this. It was basic Styrofoam plates, stainless steel rectangles. And I loved the lack of pretense, of artificial decor. Let the food stand on its own, brown, watery, yet indescribably satisfying.

Little Tejas, the elf, wouldn't eat anything, though. They were all involved in one of those battle of the wills children sometimes do. He was skinny, his legs as thin as canes. Often, when I came he was seated in front of a bland mass of curds and rice, I believe the only thing he would touch. Another child, a Burmese boy, joined their little group and the mother also liked to cook. We then became a threesome, going to Helen's house to learn Burmese green curry and fried rice. I tried to think what I could teach these women, all I know are borrowed things from other cultures, and surely a Virginia ham would sicken them. Helen only used slivers of meat or ham in her fried rice and Stella ate mostly vegetarian. I had them to dinner, and tried my best, but really, in the end, it was obvious the Indian food was what we all wanted. And I worked, as if a student, on the dishes. What Stella taught me I immediately went home to reproduce. I worked on many versions of chana dal, spicy chickpea stew eaten with warm and buttery chapatis. I loved this, and tried it many times. But the chickpeas stayed hard, no matter how long I cooked them. They had been cooking for two hours when Stella arrived to pick up Tejas.

What are you doing here, she asked immediately, bending over the pot, somehow the scent alarmed her keen sense of food mastery.

I'm, you know, cooking the chana. it's still hard.

She laughed that weedling laugh, I defy you to cook it until it is soft then, she said.

Something was wrong.

What do you mean, it won't?

Did you add salt?

Of course.

Then it will never soften.

After she left, I harrumphed. Come on. But she was right, I cooked it a few more hours, mere pebbles rolling in the water. I gave up at that point, and went with canned. I still always laugh at that I defy you when I cook with chickpeas, so proud and exactly sure she was of her knowledge.

Then one day they were relocated to a hospital in Danbury, Connecticut. I was sad to have my mentor and only friend leave. We visited them maybe six months later, and Ganesh's father was living with them. Tejas was bigger. Stella said, I believe you have lost weight and I believe you have found it, she said, referring to my husband. She gave me a small picture that was always by her dresser, of a woman with a lyre, years later I realized it was Persian, a hint of things to come into my life. I never heard from her again. She could not write, in that she hadn't learned to read or write. But, occasionally, I spot the word Kerala, now represented by a woman with waist-length black hair with a slight wave, a wheedly voice, a way in the kitchen.

❖ Aloo Paratha

This is a delectable stuffed bread with a spicy potato mixture.

Filling
2 all-purpose potatoes, such as Yukon Gold, not peeled
2 to 3 tablespoons vegetable oil
1 teaspoon black mustard seeds
½ teaspoon ground turmeric
6 curry pata leaves
1 teaspoon ground ginger
1 small green chile, chopped
½ teaspoon salt
3 to 4 teaspoons chopped fresh cilantro

Bread
1 tablespoon oil, plus some for frying
3 teaspoons salt
3 large handfuls chapati whole wheat flour (buy at Indian
    food store or use regular whole wheat flour)

To prepare filling, boil potatoes until soft. Let cool slightly. Peel and mash roughly in a bowl. Heat oil in a pan, add mustard seeds, and cook until they pop. Immediately add turmeric, curry pata, ginger, chile, and salt. Sauté briefly and add to potato mixture. Add cilantro and mix well. Let cool.

To make the bread, mix oil, salt, and flour until the mixture resembles cornmeal. Add cold water until a light dough forms, and knead for about 5 minutes.

Place some flour on work surface. Remove enough dough to make a ball about 2 inches in diameter. Roll into a circle by rolling on all sides rapidly, and make very flat. Place 2 tablespoons filling inside and wrap four sides of dough over filling. Quickly roll out bread to flatten. Do the same with remaining dough. Heat oil on a griddle or in paratha pan over medium-high heat. Fry breads on griddle until brown spots appear, and then flip them over to brown on the opposite side. Fry all the breads in this manner. Keep them warm in oven.

Chapter 15

Writing and Cooking

More Similar Than You Think

Everybody has a story they want to tell. I hear this every day, I've got a great book right here, they'll say, pointing to their head. Or, do I have a story for you, they'll exclaim devilishly. Great, I'll answer, go write it!

And that's the hard part. After a long hard day at work, after cooking dinner, drinking a beer, helping your kids with home-work, or picking them up at soccer or doing last-minute shop-ping at Costco, then you're going to write the Great American Novel? When you'd just as soon soak in a hot tub or space out in front of CNN?

Likewise, most people boast at least one recipe they make well. There are several types of people when it comes to food, at least in terms of Americans. There are the:

1) I can't even boil water variety. They seem proud of this, incidentally.

2) I only cook four things and that's it. Again, they seem resolute, and oddly proud.
3) I cook and proudly so. This person is into food, collects cookbooks, tries new stuff.
4) I cook the perfect _____ (fill in the blank). I actually kind of admire these people. They take one basic standard, like meat loaf, and test it so many times they come up with what they assume is the ne plus ultra of meatloaf. Unfortunately, they are usually stubborn about sharing the recipe. Oddly, when sampled, their baby recipe is not that good. Good cooking is not about hard work and repetition. Sometimes, just blind luck and a touch of sensibility work. And sometimes, just leave it alone.
5) One more person I just have to mention: the collector, who collects recipes and never uses them. I assume this type is a dreamer, someone who aspires to some kind of culinary flair but can't take a risk of failure.

There are similar types in writing:

1) The "I can't even write my own name" variety. They act as if what you do is akin to writing algorithms for NASA or such. They just write e-mails, they say. And badly.
2) The writers. These people write journals, "morning pages," and countless novels and short stories. They are productive. Is it mind-blowing? Not necessarily, but at least they are trying.
3) The "I just write copy for my nonprofit organization's newsletter." They act as if they are, on a daily

basis, misusing the English language, though I don't know why.

4) The "I only write poems don't know how to write a story" variety. Just do it. There is no instruction manual. Well, there are, but ignore them.

5) The perfectionist is the worst. More on them later.

I look at my students at on the first day of class and I tell them, you've committed an act of great bravery.

They look at me oddly.

You've struck out for yourself.

More blank stares.

You've decided that the internal and eternal you, the you that feels your experience in this world, is ready to speak. You've decided to be real. And you should be proud. It is not easy. You will have to dedicate, but it will bring you great joy. Most people will never take this step.

And then I see an emotion come across their faces: fear.

Where do they start? Will it be good?

I am amazed and delighted by this fear—that writing carries such power in this day and age—and yet very aware of how debilitating it can be. A new writer needs to be aware that we are in the process of workshopping—that these works should indeed be unfinished and rough. We are simply, at the beginning point, gathering faint wisps, mere shadows. Fear also propels—it can be used as a vehicle for production, as opposed to boredom.

Perfectionism really kills productivity in a writer. I try to encourage the idea that all work should saved in some format—so that writers don't panic at the idea of editing. Snippets of phrases or whole sections of text don't need to deleted, they can simply be cut and pasted to be used in the future. It is my belief that anything put to paper by the writer has the energy of importance and should be saved. You may not actually use the original language, but pay attention to the impulse— where did it come from and why was it important enough to write down?

In cooking, you have the same problem. It's just one meal, people! Don't stress about burning the salmon. Plunge in. You will only learn by touching, smelling, and tasting. Do it often. Be an active cook. Like the person who annoys all by dragging on and on in their decision of what to order in a restaurant— the menu in their face, the waiter looking at his watch—it's only one meal in a long line of millions. Take a risk.

In a sense these impulses, cooking and writing, come from the basic seed of love. We have been moved, touched by the sensual experience of a great meal, a moving book. We would like to somehow harness this power and give it to others. Good writing and good cooking are processes of uncovering. Each has a unique voice and I think it is my job (and then, theirs) to help them unleash this ability. By unleash I mean, release it from the restraints that they have bound it in. This is one area in their lives where compromise is not encouraged. You must absolutely and unequivocally do what you want. Don't think what people think. You must pay attention to your inner impulse. Don't be perfect.

Don't try and be James Beard on your first dinner-party foray! Keep it simple. Most of all, have fun. Why should this be stressful? Enjoy the beauty of your ingredients and play. Add a little white wine, rub in some rosemary. Smell the garlic (but don't let it burn, it gets bitter). The best way to cook is to start with ingredients. Like characters, these are the kingpins of your meal. A fresh tomato, for example. Next, you see that halibut is particularly fresh. You spot some lovely basil. Keep it simple. Grill the fish, toss some tomato slices with basil. It can't be better. The ingredients shine.

If you want to cook, but you are afraid, don't start out making what you had in a four-star restaurant a few months ago. Make something improvisational. A chicken soup works. Get a nice chicken, hopefully organic. Put it in a pot with some cut-up veggies of your choice. This is where it gets easy. Do what you feel like. Carrots? Sure. Onions? Absolutely. It doesn't matter. You'll learn as you go that it's best to put in potatoes later because they completely melt down after several hours of simmering the hen, thus clouding the broth, but, hey, will it taste good? Yes. And you'll learn for next time. Just let it simmer and eat it up. Keep doing it every week, and after a while, you'll know what tasted good, what works, etc. Maybe the avocados weren't a great idea. After you've enjoyed yourself, experimented, attempted something new, then, and only then, read a recipe. First, let your natural abilities fly.

I believe we all have the ability to tell good stories, that wonderful writers lie in all students. It is a psychological process whereupon one sheds ego and unleashes an energy within themselves they didn't realize existed. You have to learn to unlearn, to paraphrase Picasso, and be a child again. Or, damn it, get in the kitchen. Enjoy life. Cook a meal. Start remembering what you ate as a child, ask people what they ate. Their stories start to tumble out as quickly as the memories of food, because they are all intertwined, food and memory, love and taste, all piecemeal of this lovely, sensual world we live in.

Chapter 16

Kousa and Warak

Memories and Food

A new recipe like this, kousa and warak, promises much to me. It will involve the senses, of course, but somehow I will be entering the delicate nimbic world of memory as well: where the senses, in the realm of stimulation by food, sex, love, pain, loss, drama, meld their own tiny space in memory, a feeling space encapsulated and welded from the sense-stimulaters at the moment. This recipe is from a student of mine who generously lent it to me. He had mentioned it in a short story in the class I teach, about a boy living in Lebanon during the seventies, and war. In some sense, I imagine, this represents perhaps his mother, his family, the apartment in Lebanon, his grandmother. It must also though taste of war in the faintest essence. To me as I make it, it will be flavored by the music in my house, my dog, my children, the atmosphere of my feelings right now, divorced, confused, hungry, passionate. I will taste it with my own memories, but his will also be there. I will be tasting a piece of his life, as will you by reading this and sensing the experience. You may try this recipe in your own home and think of tragedy, like a war, and of family joy and warmth, and as you taste the warak, you will be spreading the energy of this recipe.

There is another recipe in this book, khoresht bademjoon, which is Persian eggplant and lamb stew, and I've included this one, because recipes can also be all about love, and love comes from the stomach in a such a visceral way. I had a Persian boyfriend for a couple of years, and I made this for him. I practiced and practiced, and added input, or others did—and I tasted it at people's houses and finally I got it right, so right that he would taste it in shock. It was better than his mother's, he said. It became the undoing of that man, the final nail in the crucification of love. When someone can reproduce your child's delighted mouth, what can you do, but roll on the floor and give up?

❖ Zucchini and Stuffed Grape Leaves

2 pounds small zucchini
One 16-ounce jar grape leaves
1 cup uncooked short-grain rice
2 sticks margarine or butter
1 pound ground beef
4 teaspoons salt (or to taste)
2 tablespoons ground cinnamon
2 tablespoons ground nutmeg
2 tablespoons ground allspice
1 beef bouillon cube
Lemon salt to taste (optional)

Kousa and Warak

Clean zucchini and hollow out. Dip grape leaves in hot water to rinse off the preservatives. Set aside in a colander to drain. Soak rice in boiling water. Melt margarine in a cake pan over a low fire. Season meat with salt and spices.

Mix rice, meat, and margarine together with hands . . . still over the low fire. The meat will not be completely cooked. Stuff zucchini and grape leaves with mixture. To stuff leaves, spread one leaf out, put a small amount of rice and meat mixture in middle. Roll up, folding sides in as you go. Put all in a pressure cooker (zucchini on the bottom). Cover with hot water seasoned with a bouillon cube, and lemon salt if you like. Water should be just one finger below the top of the vegetables. If using a regular pan, completely cover with water. Cook 20 to 25 minutes in pressure cooker or 1½ hours in pan. Let cooker open by itself. Good with yogurt.

Mom doesn't make it much, because preparing the warak is incredibly *painstaking work, hours of rolling and stuffing. But it's the food of the gods.*

Did your grandmother make doughnuts, and shake them in a brown paper bag, with sugar? give someone the recipe and they know your grandmother, with her youthful figure in a print dress, shaking the sugar in the bag, watching the street from her window in the morning, steam from a laundry shop rising in the air.

Did your father make riceballs for picnics? Did you make them stuffed with sour plums, and taste and see your father's quiet face as you made them, watching the springtime on a picnic when you were five?

When it's over, when life is over, we can't eat. We are full. There is no need anymore. When someone leaves you and you are in pain, you can't eat. When you are sick, you can't eat.

When you are in surgery, or worried, or when you are very poor, you can't eat.

But when you are living life, your senses are alive. You eat, you laugh. You cry. but you eat. When people attend funerals, they eat desperately, almost in a rage against life.

Chapter 17

Yesterday and Today, and So Forth

Although I write, I am still consumed by cooking. What did I do yesterday instead of finishing this book? I cooked.

Grilled Sirloin in a Bordelaise Sauce
Roulade of Pork with Rosemary, Pear, and Ginger
    Chutney
Twice-Baked Potatoes
Creamed Spinach

I know, I know—steakhouse menu circa 1954, except for the chutney, which is more 1988. This was for private-chef clients. Twice a week, I deliver food for which I have carefully shopped, a menu I created from old cookbooks or scouring the food blogs or most likely, from what looks good in the market. I deliver it to my lovely clients who shall remain nameless, but they are wonderful folks who live in a luxurious English apartment they built in the middle of their enormous horse coliseum—yes, they live in a barn. But not a drafty barn, a sumptuous and elegant barn, why these horses live better than most people in the world. And these clients just want high-quality food for the week, not restaurant food, but real food, lovingly crafted. They don't care what I serve, in fact they prefer not to approve any menus or have any say at all. No veal. No grouper. Other than that, go wild.

Sometimes I feel an Asian mood, and we'll have green curry with prawns, Thai cucumber salad, shrimp and pork dumplings, yum nua (grilled beef salad with nuoc cham dressing and ground roasted rice powder).

Here's another sample menu:

Wild Steelhead Salmon with Lentils
Chicken Fricassee with Chicken Chorizo
Homemade Italian Meatloaf
Roasted Delicata Squash
Cold Avocado Soup
Stewed Kale

I still cater as well. I do weddings and lunches, cocktail parties, weaving these activities around my writing. When I cook for people, I adjust around their tastes, energy, personalities. Food is to please. For my children, I roast chicken, grill steak. Or, I make a hearty minestrone. They like Korean barbecue, sushi, Persian kebab, even Ethiopian. And McDonald's. They are kids, after all. For my friends and family, I have stored their food choices on a mental Rolodex for use at any time.

My mother: I would say she favors French cheese, rich risottos, sparkling fresh sushi, any and all seafood, rich red wine and chocolate.

My stepfather has his odd quibbles: no tarragon, no cinnamon. Non-mushy.

My father, Mark: anything ethnic, spicy, and again, seafood. Condiments.

My brother: rustic and satisfying, stews, a hunk of cheese and good bread. Again, seafood. No eggplant, makes his ears itch. Can't handle meat that is too raw.

And me: I wobble all over the place. When I am alone, I shop with glee for all the odd whims—fumy bleu cheeses, gooey chèvres, smoked fish, super rare beef. Oysters. Good yogurt. Nuts. At times I crave greens sautéed in garlic or weird things like liver, sweetbreads, kidneys. And sometimes, when I am completely spent, burned out: Quality thin spaghetti tossed with aglio-olio. And if I'm becoming sick, boiled potatoes. And then, sometimes, I must have slabs of toro and sake or quormeh sabzi.

Writing makes me hungry. There is not a moment that food is not on my mind, on some level. Whether I am preparing to cook for my client's weekly food, like tomorrow, or making dinner for my children, like tonight, I am thinking of menus. My whole life is a menu of some sort. Tonight I will be grilling steak, served with roasted potatoes, a light salad, nothing extraordinary because my children like this meal. Tomorrow I will make a Catalonian chicken stew, perhaps a cool cucumber soup, Moroccan carrots for my clients.

My ex-husband, Russell, collects lists, strewn on floors or found in shopping carts. They are little works of art, a tiny snapshot of a life. I've started picking them up, too. They have their poetry. First of all, you notice the choice of paper. Sometimes, it's children's looseleaf, which they pilfered from a notebook lying on the kitchen table. Other times, it's torn from a small memo pad with kittens on the top or a humorous cartoon or a monogram. Orderly types have printed it out from the computer. Sometimes the handwriting is a scrawl, other times a controlled cursive. I find that some people have the same thing every night of the week. Other times, there are only the essentials scrawled, wine, tampons, half-and-half.

I've lost many of these lists as well, but they have mostly been long, scratched-out catering lists that go on and on. I wonder if anyone has read these mini books of mine. They are here and there, in the car, in my purse, left in carts, small snapshots of a brief moment of my life, in shorthand.

I did this party not too long ago. It is easy to make things sound bucolic and sweet, but there were many undercurrents at this party, as with all of them. Everything is a story unfolding. The hostess had promised us her garden workers would be there to set up the tables and chairs, but they unexpectedly didn't show up because it was grape-picking season (we live in a land of vineyards). So my staff, just three of us, had to set up everything and we were desperately running out of time. We had to set up the grills as well. Roberto called in two women he knew, I met them in the local town, they flew in and started cranking open the tables. The hostess had decided to do her own decorating and flowers, and one hour before the party, she still had buckets of flowers all over the tables and floors, and odd, assorted vases in piles. It was a mess. The grills hadn't been started. She also had bags of candles still wrapped in plastic. The bartender limped around because he had gout, and couldn't really work, there were many levels of stone patios he had to circumvent and he was getting cranky and irritated opening the tables. The daughter of the hostess, as dark-eyed as a Sicilian, with long tresses, wrapped in a shawl, took to drinking huge glasses of vodka. After one whole bottle, we were alarmed. An Irish three-part band arrived and set up. There would be a champagne toast in time to the sunset and since this was on a lovely farm, the sky was becoming salmon tinted against the lush trees. The candles seemed to appear on the tables covered magically in cloths. My brother was the chef, he was in a cloud of smoke grilling the butterflied lamb. The bartender had opened his wine and set up glasses. The flowers were done. People started drifting in, seeking a drink. The music started up, a whinnying fiddle. The party had begun. All was well and forgotten.

Chapter 18

The Last Course

This book starts and ends in the farmlands of Virginia. Although sometimes we travel here and there, in the end we are always still in the place where we lived as a child, metaphorically or physically. It is that strange house you inhabited as a child, created of the sensations and thoughts around you, that you always carry.

I am still there. As a child, my friends at the private school I attended frolicked with large color TVs, Go-Karts, ponies, and swimming pools, I had the open air, dirt, dried locusts by the thousands underneath buckeye trees, Country Joe and the Fish, Jimi Hendrix and Janis Joplin with the R. Crumb album cover I studied for hours. My brother John and I cooked for entertainment as children, especially omelettes and candied mint leaves. There was endless downtime. There are no camps, piano lessons to mar the stretch of morning to afternoon. I spent my time drawing in small journals I kept by the pound, or reading every book lining the shelves, regardless of content. Or fishing. Dabbling in paints. In the corner of my eye, long hair, bangs, miniskirts or Moroccan kaftans, beads, incense. I used to love Leonard Cohen. And Bob Dylan always played somewhere, his wail was a backdrop.

And I loved my grandparents, who lived next door. I teeter-tottered between the scrappy living-off-the-land existence in my house and their elegant mansion surrounded by boxwood, as if we were the sharecroppers. And she is a writer who wrote alone on her large white chenille bed every afternoon, long-hand on her manila pads. I was forbidden to enter those quarters then and on some level, that defined who I am, someone always on the outskirts, the edge, looking in. A few lone times I made it to the top and was strangely welcomed by my grand-mother, a few times I was caught halfway and banished to the mudroom. And, in essence, there are times when I fit in society, perhaps when I was married, but most times, I am comfortable as a peripheral player. I like to observe, to watch. I am scared to intrude.

So, to pass the time—and it always seemed like there was endless time to pass, as if I was always waiting—my brother John and I hung out with my teenaged uncle, downstairs. He'd play his albums over and over. He told us that a ghost lives in the attic named Boo Radley and I believed him. I thought I saw him once. Years later, I realize it's a character out of a book.

My father, Mark, divorced from Ann, is a photographer and writer in Washington, D.C. He had a gallery with a friend. He often wrote art pieces, or critiques for the *Washington Post* or the front of show catalogues and as a child I read them and tried to figure out what the heck he was saying, the words so arcane and intelligent, again, I noted that being a writer was an impossibility for me, obviously. I was more concerned with in-venting Barbie-Ken vignettes than debating photographic jux-tapositions (he liked that word). He had written a novel, when he was young, though he couldn't get it published. He said his agent lost the only copy. (The sound of John Coltrane. Your father heard him live in clubs in New York in the sixties.)

His father, my grandfather, had written a book, published by William Sloane Associates in 1950 called *The Encounter,* the story of a priest's run-in with the tawdry world of carnival tradesmen. I devoured that book and it left me in awe. It still does. I found a handwritten note by him on the back of a bank statement in the copy I have, a bound first edition, and he wrote: "As an experiment, The Encounter was intended to be a modernist version of an anecdote from Rufinus of Aquileia (ca. 400 a.d.) relating an incident alleged to have occurred to Paphnutius, a celebrated monk and ascetic of the Egyptian Thebaid, who at his own request is shown by an angel his equal in merit, a man who is a vagrant flute-player and ex-robber."

This man, Francis Power, my grandfather, is an aesthete who lives in a baroque house in the countryside, Yale educated, a Catholic scholar, architect, writer, perfume maker, and gourmand whose study is lined with ancient tomes of rare books and a human skull. Throughout his life I heard he was working on a history of stone church architecture, and I remember, vividly, his ascots, his fine silk Italian robe (which I inherited) and the fact he smoked a cigarette from a holder. It was his copy, a first edition, of *Against Nature* by J. K. Huysmans (considered a Bible of fin-de-siècle decadence) that influenced you so as a teenager, in his patchouli-drenched study. I would never pretend to being a writer like that. You did not go to Yale.

(He liked the music of Kurt Weill.)

And my mother: is there a subject she is not interested in? She is an explorer, my mother. Every year she will discover and interpret a new thought, new food, new worlds, and bring them to us. Right now she is a planning commissioner, saving our lovely county from destruction by overzealous developers. She has been a teacher of special education and a realtor. I believe she could be anything, any time, she is a changeling. One had to be in this family. And God knows she can cook anything. My brother is a chef, I mentioned before, and he too was trained in the early years by a mere lack of anything else to do.

My maternal grandfather, Gene, "Golly," husband of the writing grandmother, went to Princeton and worked at Charles Scribner and Sons during the Maxwell Perkins days. He read the manuscripts of Fitzgerald, Hemingway, and Faulkner, he told me, and saw Hemingway while on honeymoon in Key West, who was drunk and punched someone in a bar. He is a great storyteller and even at eighty-six, he tended to make women swoon. This only adds to your feeling that writers are mythological and different from average people. His son, my uncle Harrison, publishes a fine story in *Sewanee Review*, which everyone says is a fine literary magazine. You read it and it is indeed masterful.

(Your grandfather can sing velvety renditions of "Stardust" and Cole Porter, etc. He could've been a singer, with that voice and the dark looks, though it was probably not of his social calling.)

At Bennington, later on, you finally do take a writing workshop, but my friend, who introduces you to Thomas Mann and who writes that well (you think), says casually that you can never write. As casually as if discussing the lineup at the cafeteria that night. You realize you have made a huge mistake and stop. You think of the real writers. You go back to drawing and cooking, your œuvres.

(Bennington College in 1981 frolicked with Ska and New

Wave, young painting students wore vintage clothes and flung their bodies around at the Dressed to Get Laid parties.)

For years I have a catering business. I spend way too much time writing the menus with fabulist, euphemistic descriptions meant to evoke other eras but you wonder if clients really like that. Is a Spit-Roasted Wild-Rosemary and Lavender-Fed Free Range Loudoun County Hen better than herbed chicken? I decide to take a writing workshop, just for fun. In the class, the teacher is too encouraging. I freakishly start a novel, with the devil-may-care attitude someone might attempt to find a cure for cancer in their garage. To my shock, no one has acted particularly revolted by your work, therefore I take a few more classes, but you do not worry about publishing because that is an impossibility, only suddenly a fever takes hold of you and you can't stop, writing becomes some sort of addiction and next thing you know, to your surprise and embarassment, you've published a book.

(Most of the aforementioned works of music now have become odd passkeys to memory, and you use them as such, unlocking and drafting feelings lost through the years, as if method acting. The older you get, the more beloved and frail those memories become, losing resentment like dye fades from fabric.)

Being on the outskirts of this phenomenal family made me write. This I felt comfortable doing. I had no other goal or even ability. In the beginning of my connection, I somehow felt in. But slowly through the years, I could feel distinctly the disconnect. That somehow, even though we were blood, I did not fit in this group of people as charming, intelligent, and as attractive as they were: I was not one of them. Perhaps it wasn't just me, maybe that is why my mother pulled out as well.

I was accepted for a while, but I somehow departed. I don't know if I did it or it was done. Maybe it started when Owen lost his mind in those early days. Maybe the safe family, so full of laughter, seemed suddenly ominous. Or, when I moved to Greenwood when Ann and John married, did I lose my connection then? Yes, in a sense we had pulled away. Or, a nasty blow, when my grandparents and all the rest, uncles and his family, did not come to my wedding, inexplicably, and through all the excuses—we'll be in Maine, then!, etc.—was it because he was Jewish? Regardless, it was another loosening of the screws, another tiny loss. An then, between the fights and silence between my mother and them, we (Ann, John, my brother, and me), the final finials gave way and the worlds cracked away from each other. I was now on the outside. I was back on the stairs, hovering outside the door, waiting for an entry. There is no place to put these feelings of loss, because it just is. It is over, us. There is still love on all sides, just confusion and ineptitude.

But I'm not the only one.

This is a family that doesn't know how to deal.

There are many of us, but one comes to mind. He sits in a room in Richmond. They say he has a cassette player, that someone gave him the *White Album*, which they play for him. He was obese for years, lack of exercise, and medications did this, along with institutional foods, until now, strangely, he has lost it all and is lean and in his face is the old Owen, with black hair streaked with gray and blue eyes. Nancy brings him clothes a couple of times a year, so he sits politely in a blue oxford shirt and khakis. They told him Gene had died, and he was silent. He watches TV. He used to be a problem with the nurses, he would sometimes try to touch them, but he has stopped. He

was a very good golf player as a young man who could beat Gene, who was the master. But he doesn't do that anymore. We could visit him. I've thought about it. I've thought, I really should. But I remember the days in Crednal, at his house, as a young girl, and how I became scared of him. And I imagine him being angry or breaking out and chasing me and my children down, hurting us, maybe irrational, but still, powerful. And I do nothing. And just like everyone in this family, it is too uncomfortable, too weird for me to deal with, so I move on, ignore and pretend everything is okay.

And Nancy, she is alone in a home in Charlottesville. Every week I want to visit her. I did last year or was it the year before? But I am afraid. I do not know why. I am afraid to face the pain she has from everybody, Owen, Ann, me, from not visiting her. I am afraid she will think I am fat. I am afraid of everything. This is not a lack of love. It's just that love can't fix everything. I will visit her. I will soon. I will not visit Owen. But I will remember him, especially when I hear "Yesterday."

In the meantime, I can plan for Christmas Eve because this year I will make something special, something unique: I will make Carrie's stuffed crawfish, and cracked conch. And yellow bird cocktails. And maybe, as a joke, the apricot chicken. And we can make toasts and throw the glasses in the fireplace. And I'll bring the soundtrack, the Stones, the Beatles.

And then, we can laugh laugh laugh.

About the Author

Nani Power is the author of *Crawling at Night, The Good Remains,* and *The Sea of Tears,* the first two of which were picked as *New York Times* Notable Books of the Year. She lives in Virginia.